Flight from Reason

A Mother's Story of Schizophrenia, Recovery and Hope

A Memoir
Karen S. Yeiser

This is a true story. Unnecessary identifying information about people and institutions that played a part in this story has been withheld in order to protect privacy.

www.karensyeiser.com

This book contains the poem "Perhaps She Will Land upon That Shore" from the book Prodigals and Those Who Love Them by Ruth Bell Graham, Published by Baker Books, a division of Baker Publishing Group, Copyright ©1991, 1999, fourth printing, November 2001. Used by permission.

Scripture quotations are taken from the Holy Bible, New Living Translation, copyright ©1996, 2004. Used by permission of Tyndale House Publishers, Inc., Wheaton, Illinois 60189. All rights reserved.

Digital Ed. ISBN 978-0-9903452-1-3
Create Space Ed. 978-0-9903452-3-7

FIRST EDITION

To my courageous daughter Bethany
And to families everywhere
who suffer the ravages of mental illness

Table Of Contents

Author's Note

It is my hope that by sharing the events in this book, you will gain increased awareness of how mental illness can silently overtake a life. If this story touches you in a positive way, or inspires even one person to make a firm commitment toward treatment and recovery, then it was worth the time and effort spent putting it together.

Foreword

There is no worse trauma to any mother than to lose a child. The author of this book, Karen, is a nurse who, with her husband, Pastor David, raised a daughter and a son in a loving and caring home in Ohio. Her daughter, Bethany, a "perfect child" according to Karen, grew up to become an academic high-achiever, an accomplished violinist, and a well-behaved, pleasant young lady. Karen and David were delighted to see Bethany go to a major university on the West Coast on a scholarship to major in molecular biology and to pursue a career in medicine. Things went very well for about 3 years and then Bethany, following a trip to Africa, changed drastically and became obsessed with helping the poor and sick in poor countries, and her grades plummeted from As to Fs. She demanded that her parents send her money to enable her to travel to various countries on a mission to "help the poor", which they were alarmed and reluctant to do. Bethany stopped communicating with her mom and dad, who were unaware that she was developing schizophrenia, a very serious psychotic brain disorder, which causes delusions (bizarre thinking) and hallucinations (hearing voices talking to her, as well as seeing imaginary people).

Karen's peaceful world soon turned upside down. She lost contact with her daughter for the next 4 years, during which Bethany had dropped out of college, gave away all her belongings and became homeless for the next 4 years, with one dress to wear, eating discarded food from garbage cans on campus, and sleeping in the backyard of a church in a downtown area. Karen and David had no idea what happened to their beautiful and smart daughter thousands of miles away. Karen's long nightmare had begun.

In this powerful personal account of her suffering, worry, stress, and anguish over several years, when she did not know what happened to her beloved daughter, Karen eloquently and poignantly describes the details of the ordeal that she and her husband David went through while trying to find their lost daughter. It also demonstrates how, despite their sleepless nights, heavy hearts, and dark days, Karen was relentless in her pursuit of finding Bethany. For

1500 anxiety-laden days, Karen never stopped searching for any clue or lead to find her daughter's whereabouts, or whether she was dead or alive. She was completely unaware that her daughter had developed schizophrenia and was aimlessly walking around in the unsafe streets of a big city, completely under the command and control of the hallucinatory voices she was hearing, scrounging for food in trash cans, and sleeping on slabs of concrete. David flew to the West Coast city where Bethany had attended university, looking for his daughter in the big city, not deterred by the realization that it was like trying to find a needle in a haystack. It is an amazing story of determination and persistence, fueled by parental love for a daughter who vanished from their lives.

Thankfully, Karen's intensely emotional and gut-wrenching story had a happy ending but not without further heartache, when one day, she and David suddenly received a call from the police, asking them to come and see their hospitalized daughter. That's when Karen's and Bethany's journey of healing began, but it was still a long and rocky road of relapses, emergency room visits, and re-hospitalizations, before Bethany, slowly and miraculously, recovered from the disabling symptoms of schizophrenia. As Bethany's psychiatrist who provided the necessary medical care to enable her to defeat her psychosis and get rid of her hallucinations, I interacted often with Karen and David and realized what a wonderful and supportive family Bethany had, to help shepherd her back to a normal life. Family support is so critical for young people with mental illness and Bethany was truly fortunate to have that in her life because many of my patients with schizophrenia do not.

Karen's book is an inspiring message for all families, parents and their adult children. Her story is emblematic of the indomitable human spirit when guided by love and dedication. Mental health professionals such as counselors, social workers, psychologists, nurses, psychiatrists and all their trainees would find the emotional rollercoaster of Karen's experiences as a vivid example of what parents of their patients go through. For Karen and David, the wounds have now healed, but reading Karen's description, it portrays the invisible scars of their multi-year struggles to get their daughter back to sanity. With my and David's encouragement, both Karen and Bethany authored their memoirs after Bethany graduated from the University of Cincinnati (with honors), to be shared with all those who have dealt with mental illness and its challenges in their families. To me, writing down their feelings and thoughts was undoubtedly therapeutic, and a vital component of closure.

Henry A. Nasrallah, M.D.
Professor and Chairman
Department of Neurology and Psychiatry
Saint Louis University School of Medicine

Preface

Often when I am alone and have time to reflect, my mind wanders back to the years prior to becoming a mother, and even an adult. I long to once again experience the freedom of being untouched by the effects of severe mental illness. I long to erase the sorrow that echoes in the hidden places of my heart, but I know in life there is no going back.

I had no reason to believe I would ever write a memoir. The first part of my life was unexceptional. I married in my early twenties and lived in a responsible manner. I was a registered nurse, a wife, a parent, and a dependable employee. I expected both of my healthy children to live normal lives like mine, but I was wrong.

Ever so silently, schizophrenia kidnapped my talented and loving daughter and turned her into a despondent, dirty stranger living on the street. I had no idea such a thing could happen to ordinary people. But I know it now, and I want to share my story so other families can be spared the devastation that untreated mental illness can bring.

This is the true story of how I completely lost my daughter. But by the grace of God, she has returned.

Tears streamed down my face as the sad but beautiful music filled the car. My heart was broken. Beauty had twisted into ugliness. Happiness had flown away.

ONE

When Bethany was born my husband and I lived in a small one-bedroom apartment in the Chicago suburbs. When she was five weeks old we moved to a farming community. My husband, having just completed graduate school, was grateful to secure a ministerial position at a beautifully situated, historic rural church in western Illinois. Although our move took us away from family and friends, we were eager to get on with our lives.

Our new home was a two-story white farmhouse surrounded by expansive corn and soybean fields stretching as far as the eye could see. Multi-generational farm families sparsely populated the land, and our house and church were located many miles from an actual town. We were young and happy, with every reason to believe the future would bring many joys.

When we moved, I suspended my career as a registered nurse to become a stay at home mom. Freedom from a working schedule gave me countless hours to spend with Bethany. With joy we watched her grow and meet all the developmental milestones right on time.

As soon as she could sit up we began reading books to her. As months and seasons passed she smoothly transitioned from baby words to a wide functional vocabulary with remarkably good pronunciation. Her verbal skills were advanced for her young age and people began to notice.

In contrast to life in the Chicago area, we found the country to be fairly slow paced, and Bethany and I spent most of our days quietly at home. One day, when she was sixteen months old, just for a change of scenery, her father and I took her to a large enclosed shopping mall. This day specifically stands out in my memory because we bought Bethany a pair of shoes, and she was quite enthralled by the way her footsteps echoed as she ran across the shiny floors in the mall.

Later that day, while window shopping at a jewelry counter, a salesman spoke to Bethany and with clear diction she responded to him in complete sentences. He was amused that such a little person could speak so well, and called another salesman over just to listen.

We assumed her advanced speech was a result of living with two adults who did not communicate in "baby talk." She was a bright and inquisitive child, devoted to books, games, and music.

Bethany's brother was born when she was only eighteen months old, but she seemed to adjust well to this major change in our family structure. As both children grew they naturally became playmates. In early childhood they used their imaginations to make up all sorts of games and spent hours building elaborate creations out of snap-together blocks of different sizes.

The strong, continual winds of the open plains did not prevent our children from playing on the swing set in our back yard or from climbing the huge snow drifts that formed every winter, and limitless hours were spent at the kitchen table drawing stacks of pictures and creating little story books. Vivid sketches of happy people, rainbows, and flowers were recurrent themes of Bethany's artwork.

Our family had limited access to cable television programming because we lived too far from an actual town. Long days were filled by creating interesting activities and reading books. Each afternoon, both children sat with me as I read out loud their favorite titles which progressed from Little Golden Books™ to the entire set of *Little House on the Prairie* books by Laura Ingalls Wilder.

At least twice a week Bethany and her brother joined children their own age for group activities at church and in the community. As a family, we were well connected to many kind and loving people. Bethany seemed to relate well to others and enjoyed playing with friends.

From a very early age Bethany demonstrated a strong appetite for knowledge. She dearly loved piano music and cassette recordings of children's songs. The farmhouse came equipped with an ancient upright piano with an out of tune, honky-tonk sound. Bethany happily sat next to her dad as he taught her to read music and play basic tunes like "Twinkle, Twinkle Little Star." Her dad always said that it seemed as though she learned without really being taught.

As Bethany's kindergarten year approached, due to our distance from a good school, we decided to purchase a formal curriculum of basic academic material which we could teach her at home. This decision postponed her enrollment in school until the first grade. Since she had already mastered the alphabet and numbers, we believed that by keeping her home she could advance at her own pace and retain enough time to play and use her imagination every day.

From the very start, Bethany's favorite segment of the day became the time set aside for educational instruction. Although she always wanted to work beyond the suggested daily lesson plan, we limited her time to one hour each day. In group settings, we began to notice she was much more advanced than other children her age in reading and writing. She was a happy and gentle child. It was easy to love her and very rewarding to be her parent.

Our family spent a total of six years in rural Illinois. During that period of time, we experienced the love of friends, the beauty of nature, and the quiet unfolding miracle of how infancy transitions into childhood.

TWO

In the summer of 1987, just before Bethany turned six, we moved to a suburb of Cleveland, Ohio. Our move provided broader educational opportunities for both children.

The transition from a rural farming community to a suburban setting was a total change of lifestyle for our family. Many children lived in our new neighborhood and right from the start, we opened our home to our children's favorite friends. Bethany seemed to thrive.

There was a well-established private school located just a mile from our home so we enrolled Bethany. Had we remained in Illinois, her fall birthday would have placed her in first grade, but Ohio guidelines assigned her to repeat Kindergarten. But due to her advanced ability to read and write, the school chose to administer academic testing to determine if Kindergarten really was her best option. The testing results positioned Bethany at a second grade level, however, socially and developmentally, first grade was determined to be the wisest choice. Simply put, she was the youngest first grade student in her class because we moved.

Without doubt, most parents hold a snapshot in their memory from their children's first day of school. I can still see the innocence beaming from Bethany's smiling face. She was proudly dressed in a little plaid jumper and held a red lunchbox tightly in her hand. Her thick chestnut hair fell nearly to her waist in braids. She was eager and happy to start school. But within the very first weeks, we developed concerns about her social skills because she had difficulty blending in with the other children in her class.

She found it challenging to connect with established groups of children, especially on the playground. With tenuous confidence, we reminded ourselves that she was a "new kid," the youngest in her class, and was dealing with a complete change of environment and lifestyle. We also realized that most of the other children had already spent the prior year together in Kindergarten. When we consulted with her teacher, she assured us that due to Bethany's many personal attributes, she was sure to attract friends. Together we encouraged her, providing a few practical suggestions, and before long she settled in with a few gentle girls.

Because many young families attended our church, there were several children's programs. As the minister's children, Bethany and her brother quickly established close friendships within our church, and those friendships deepened as time went by.

Our back yard was a magnet for children. It contained a two-story tree house, a go-cart, and an above ground pool. Bethany and her brother spent their summer days swimming and playing with friends. In the evenings they loved to play water basketball in the pool with their dad. All sorts of creative games were devised in our yard and in the woods surrounding two sides of our house. Each day after school Bethany and her brother, along with our scruffy grey and tan dog, Sparky, headed outside to play until the sky grew dark and they had to come inside. As parents of two healthy children, we had little to worry about and everything to be thankful for.

Bethany developed into an exceptionally well-spoken and polite child. During a few of her grammar school years, she was chosen to represent her school in an annual district-wide speech competition. This privilege involved extensive memorization and faultless recitation of literary passages. Bethany's remarkable memorization skills enabled her to retain relatively large amounts of text at a young age.

In the areas of music and academics, Bethany attracted special attention from her teachers. She had a strong desire to learn and spent time on the playground and after classes seeking them out to ask questions. Her pursuit of knowledge often expanded beyond the class lessons and textbooks. She established herself as an ideal student and was awarded "Good Citizen" certificates at the conclusion of each school year. We were thankful for the many devoted and gifted educators who demonstrated a genuine interest in her life.

At home, Bethany enthusiastically drew us into debates centered on the current topics she was studying. One night at the dinner table she dropped a firm, "grammatical truth" upon us. With authority in her voice, she declared there was no sentence in the English language beginning with the word "me." Her brother, who did not appear to be listening or have any interest in the topic, without even looking up said: "Me Tarzan." For a split second Bethany opened her mouth to rebut him... then we all doubled over with laughter.

Throughout elementary school, she advanced her piano skills with seemingly little effort on her part. She was self-motivated and loved to practice. At age seven, a friend of the family offered to give her violin lessons in our home. Bethany eagerly embraced the opportunity. We were fortunate to secure a high quality three-quarter sized violin for her which had rich and mellow tones, so she sounded quite good right from the start. Her memorization skills equipped her to fly through the basic violin books. As we attended periodic violin recitals with other children, it became clear that her technical ability was developing at a very rapid pace.

In the music world, age seven was considered to be a late start for violinists. Right from the beginning Bethany was measured against children who had begun playing at age three and had already completed four full years of instruction. We encouraged her to establish daily practice habits, and as her skills rapidly developed she became fervently self-motivated. She gained true enjoyment from mastering assigned pieces and swiftly advanced into complicated music. As she progressed through a series of very fine violin teachers, we replaced her beginner violin with a full-sized, more expensive student instrument. At a young age, violin became the central and driving passion of Bethany's life.

In sixth grade, Bethany made a decision to become a more serious, committed student. With an enormous amount of drive, she expanded and intensified her academic study time as well as her violin practice sessions. Her self-imposed standards were high and she seemed to thrive on competing with others.

In junior high school her proficiency level allowed her to enter competitions with other young violinists. Even as a small child she demonstrated a very strong competitive nature, which was often seen while playing board games such as *Monopoly* and *Scrabble*. As she matured, violin competition became strongly appealing, and fueled an expansion of her daily practice sessions.

When her competition performances fell short of her expectations, despite some tears, she seemed to logically process her feelings and set new goals. Although it was hurtful not to win, Bethany was never one to become overly emotional, collapse into despair, or lose heart.

Beyond the realm of extensive daily practice sessions and violin competition, she was regularly invited to perform for weddings, funerals and special events. She seemed happiest when sharing her music with others.

With two vibrant, growing children, our lives were packed with activities and commitments. The years blended into each other and flew by with amazing speed.

When both of our children were enrolled in school I found employment as a part-time clinic nurse in a day program for developmentally disabled adults. Before accepting this position I had very limited exposure to people with any type of disability. The tremendous responsibility greatly broadened my perspective on life. Initially, as I became acquainted with the individuals in my care, I found myself imagining what their lives could have been if only they had not become disabled. In my heart I grieved for them. One day, while trying to make sense of it all, I realized that if I was going to honestly value and treasure each person, I needed to view them as unique and special *because* of their disability. This was a turning point which allowed me to view life in a whole new light.

My nursing position granted me the privilege of watching the lives of exceptional people. Throughout the years I witnessed many people struggle just to engage in the most basic activities of daily life. Over time I began to isolate two key ingredients that stood out from all the rest as foundational in being truly happy. Those two ingredients are, being loved and accepted for who you are, and having a meaningful reason to get out of bed each day.

Even though working with the disabled helped me grow as a person and taught me new things every day, I was always thankful to return to my home knowing I had two healthy children *without* disabilities.

THREE

Upon entering high school, Bethany's drive to succeed greatly accelerated. She steadily competed against other high-achieving students for class rank. Late at night we would often see her bedroom light on and find her fast asleep in bed with an open textbook next to her.

Her violin skills developed to the point where one of the most skilled and sought after teachers in the Cleveland area accepted her as a student. At the recommendation of her new teacher, we purchased a more expensive violin and bow which produced beautiful sound. Bethany mercilessly drove herself to practice up to six hours each day after school to assure herself she was well prepared for lessons and special technique classes. She was accepted into one of the finest youth orchestras in the Midwest. The orchestra practiced and performed in Severance Hall, the home of the Cleveland Orchestra. She also joined other musicians in quartets and played violin for our Sunday church services.

Bethany structured her free time with a tight schedule of academic study, violin practice, and piano. She also taught herself basic Greek because she enjoyed the challenge of learning a new language. Through the years our family became acquainted with many individuals from different parts of the world and Bethany demonstrated great interest in learning about their unique cultures and customs.

As much as we encouraged her to set aside time for friendships, she was too goal oriented to develop much interest in typical teenage activities. When we discussed the importance of free time, she cited the practical aspect of how her hard work would pay off later in life with scholarships and special opportunities. If we pressed the point, she shut us down after engaging us in a frustrating debate, and in a way her declarations seemed fairly logical. But despite her self-discipline and achievement, we felt uneasy about her rigid schedule and her extremely limited time to just enjoy life. Our concerns began to cast a shadow over our normal daughter.

As a teenager, Bethany lived away from home for six weeks during three of her summers in order to attend an advanced violin school. Following her departure, we noticed the stress level in our home dropped significantly. She had so much energy that it seemed to radiate from her.

Bethany worked hard to earn the invitation to attend the summer violin program and we were grateful she had the opportunity to develop close friendships with other like-minded, competitive musicians. However, the environment was very competitive.

At the end of her very first week in the summer program we stopped by to visit and immediately sensed that things were not quite right. Bethany seemed stressed-out and appeared to have lost some weight. Our first impulse was to take her home, but she was intent on staying. She argued against our concerns, citing an unappetizing menu and difficulty sleeping due to performance pressure in her peer review classes. She was mortified that we would even think about taking her home. She bargained for one more week to adjust, and then assured us she would settle in and thrive. Throughout the week we monitored her through phone conversations.

When we visited her at the end of the week she seemed better adjusted and more relaxed. During the remaining weeks we attended a few student concerts which were open to the public. By attending these concerts, we were able to assure ourselves that she was coping. She settled in, and the violin school became one of her favorite experiences.

Typically during our annual family vacations, Bethany brought along her violin and a stack of study books. One summer she brought sample tests for the SAT college entry test and spent time studying while the rest of us simply unwound and enjoyed the beach. She seemed most satisfied when following a disciplined and rigorous schedule and working toward her academic and musical goals.

When she returned home, despite her tight schedule, Bethany found time to play her violin for elderly people who lived in a local nursing home. She also gave private violin and piano lessons to a few children. She spent time showing kindness to other people, but at the same time allowed herself limited opportunities to relax and enjoy the little things in life.

Her daily practice sessions continued to be long and rigorous. Every evening after dinner violin music floated down the stairs from her bedroom, so it was easy to get a feeling for just how well she thought each session was going. She had a series of mirrors over her bedroom dresser in order to check her technique, so she typically stood in the same spot when she practiced. As she pulled her bow over the violin strings, her body swayed in a back and forth motion which generated a peculiar squeak in the floor boards. The sound resonated downward through the ceiling of the living room and kitchen area and became part of the ambiance of our home. Her music was a dynamic force which could be heard and felt. She would practice for a few hours and then, just like clockwork, she would appear downstairs holding her violin and bow in pursuit of her dad who was usually willing to play the piano accompaniment to whatever piece she was working on. Our dog Sparky knew the routine. He listened from under the piano bench while the violin and piano blended together, filling the whole house with vibrant sound.

Our son brought a steady stream of friends through our home and occasionally one of them would ask why we always played a radio tuned to loud classical music behind the closed door of an upstairs bedroom. They seemed surprised when we explained it was live music as Bethany was practicing her violin. There was no way you could *not* notice her music. Sometimes just to vary her routine, she would take a break and play classical music on the piano.

Only on rare occasions would Bethany join us on the couch to watch a TV show. She was always in a hurry to get back to studying or practicing. When she did join us, it was usually because she was enticed by a program that involved science or history. Once in a while she paused long enough to enjoy a show with humor or witty dialogue. Only intellectually stimulating programming captured her attention for more than a few minutes at a time, with the exception of Christmas holiday specials.

Christmas was Bethany's favorite holiday. She loved everything about it. Each year we transformed our home, inside and out, with lights and decorations. It was typical for a Cleveland snow to arrive right on time, creating a winter wonderland. Our church always held a Christmas Eve service, and afterwards we invited special friends into our home for food and fun. Bethany would dress up and play her violin for candlelight carols. Her face glowed in the soft light as she played familiar Christmas music from memory.

One year our son received a guitar for Christmas as he had an interest in learning to play. A few hours after he received the guitar, Bethany studied the enclosed instructional booklet, tuned the instrument, learned some chords and began playing the song *O Christmas Tree*. Because she was a little slow at finding and fingering the chords, her rendition of the song was the saddest, slowest *O Christmas Tree* we had ever heard. We all laughed together as she entertained us.

A humorous quick wit was a facet of Bethany's intelligence, and when she took time to relax it was very enjoyable to be with her. Sometimes in the evening after work we felt guilty for not making the most of every minute like she did. Her drive to succeed left the rest of us feeling like a bunch of slugs and couch potatoes when we spent time watching television. She valued each day as a sacred gift which could not be wasted in her quest to advance her skills and knowledge.

The common theme in all of Bethany's interests was her fiercely competitive nature. But even though she loved competition, she chose not to participate in team sports. Instead, when given the opportunity, she loved to swim and could beat most people at table tennis. Sometimes we wondered if she enjoyed the sheer beauty of the music she played and the math, science, and languages she studied, or if she simply strove to win.

Our son was very much like other boys his age and somewhat the opposite of Bethany. He spent a lot of time skateboarding with friends and worked a part-time job. He had an advanced understanding of technical things such as car engines and electric motors which often captured his attention for hours on end. He was a good student but did not share Bethany's passionate academic drive. Despite their differences, the two of them enjoyed a good relationship with each other throughout high school. As they matured and pursued their own interests they encouraged and respected one another.

Bethany had no interest in working a part-time job. She rationalized her decision by pointing out how she could earn much more college tuition money by spending her time studying and winning scholarships than she could by working a minimum wage job. She was driven to grasp every possible educational advantage for her future and did this with seemingly endless energy and an iron will to excel.

In a way, Bethany did not dwell in the present. Even in her early teenage years she was eager to put high school behind her and loved to talk about the realm of higher education. Her focus was on the future she was building for herself. This futuristic perspective motivated her to research some of the finest universities in the United States. She had particular interest in music programs, and often questioned adults about schools they formerly attended. She was eager to spend time with young professionals and learn about their field of study.

As time passed, she began to meet many of her goals. Her grades were at the top in every school subject. She absorbed material and digested it until she had a full grasp of concept and content. This made her an exceptionally good teacher who could translate the most complicated concepts into simpler terms to match the educational level of the listener.

By the end of tenth grade, Bethany had been inducted into the National Honor Society and had exhausted the academic resources of the private school she attended, so we looked for other options. What we found was the Post-Secondary Educational Option or PSEO. State funding was made available for high school students to enroll early in college classes while simultaneously receiving high school and college credit. Since there was a community college located just one mile from our home, we explored this option. We discussed the social aspects of leaving the high school setting as well as leaving classmates she had known since first grade. The opportunity was very attractive to her as the college course offerings listed several advanced math and language classes which were not available in her high school. The opportunity would also offer her the chance to adjust to college level classes while still living in our home. Once again we were in the position of weighing Bethany's scholastic desires and needs vs. her age, as she would begin college classes just prior to turning sixteen. After much discussion about the pros and cons she decided to apply to the community college, was accepted, and enrolled with a full time load of classes.

As classes started in the fall of 1997, Bethany struggled a bit while transitioning into the community college. My husband and I began to wonder if the right decision had been made, as she experienced some tearful emotions, but after a few weeks she settled in and held fast to her choice of attending the college. Although a few friends from her private school eventually joined her, she mainly lived in a world of older commuter students. As parents we questioned whether it was the right place for her. Bethany chose not to look back and made a successful adjustment.

Early on, a college math professor recognized her proficiency and suggested she tutor engineering students in advanced math. She turned down the opportunity because she would have been assisting young men and women in their early to mid-twenties. The professor had not realized Bethany was only sixteen. We encouraged her to consider a math major, but the violin remained her passion.

Due to her more flexible school schedule, about once a month, her dad treated her to lunch at a favorite restaurant downtown after her violin lesson. They would talk about economics, politics, religion, and life goals . . . anything and everything was up for discussion. Her dad was often impressed by the depth of understanding she possessed in many subjects and he regularly commented on how much he treasured the special hours spent with her.

Because Bethany invested quite a bit of time preparing for standardized college testing, she earned a high SAT score. This achievement generated a constant stream of information from the best universities in the country who were interested in recruiting her as a student. Each day she was eager to see what the mail had brought her.

A University on the West Coast and one in the Southwest quickly became her first and second choices. Both schools offered exceptional opportunity for advancement on the violin along with very impressive academic standing. We had concerns about our daughter living so far away from us and attempted to steer her toward one of the fine universities closer to our home, but she was not interested.

We scheduled trips to visit her top two choices in order to get a feel for campus life at each university. Acceptance into music schools at the university level is by audition. Students are accepted by individual professors. An excellent audition could result in a personal invitation to study music at the university. It was a high-stakes game because in most cases a less than excellent audition would result in a rejection letter. Through the years I had witnessed several students waiting to enter performance rooms before auditions and had sensed the intense performance stress radiating from the students. I could almost physically feel their agony. If a student did not perform well during audition, they were not only rejected by the specific violin professor, but by the entire school of music because professors were the gatekeepers.

As audition dates drew closer, instead of furiously practicing like we expected, Bethany seemed to shut down a bit. We had all heard horror stories about university level auditions and wondered how Bethany would handle the high stress. We never expected her to *decrease* her practice time. Her response to the upcoming auditions made no sense to us. When we questioned her about it she became emotionally "touchy." We were worried but gave her space to manage in her own way.

During the trip to her top choice university on the West Coast, she fell in love with the school and the campus. Despite her less than expected preparation time, her audition went fairly well. She seemed to have her heart set on attending the university.

Her audition went even better at her second choice university in the Southwest. Upon her return home, Bethany anxiously awaited responses from both universities.

Soon after, Bethany was notified by phone that she was accepted by the violin professor in the Southwest, but rejected by the violin professor on the West Coast.

She was very disappointed to have lost her opportunity to study in the school of music at her first choice university. Then she made a decision that really surprised us. Despite her passion for the violin, she suddenly changed her major from music to science in order to attend the university located on the West Coast. She declared her interest in the sciences and the goal of one day becoming a doctor.

Other parents had warned us that the senior year could feel like being strapped into a death-defying roller coaster ride, but despite the warnings we were astounded. Her sudden change of plans, which placed academics higher than music, was a decision we had not anticipated. But, with all things considered we came to see her decision to be quite sensible. A major in the area of science was a practical choice and would offer many opportunities. Actually, we were relieved to see her choose a field of study not dependent on singular performances and unpredictable judges. Bethany decided to keep violin as a hobby and planned to join an orchestra, as she enjoyed performing with other musicians and wished to maintain her technical skills.

She formalized her acceptance into her first choice university on the West Coast and was granted a Presidential Scholarship which combined with our substantial monthly financial support would allow her to attend the university for at least the first year without taking a student loan. She completed her PSEO community college classes with a 4.0 grade point average. A newspaper article and picture of Bethany with two other PSEO students appeared in our local newspaper describing their outstanding scholastic accomplishments.

At a high school graduation reception for family and friends, Bethany decided to give a violin concert. She selected classical and contemporary pieces and found new energy for practicing her violin. Family members came in from out of town and our church was filled with about two hundred people who supported her. She wore a long floral dress and her hair was pulled back in a ponytail which nearly reached her waist.

Happiness and confidence radiated from her throughout an entire hour of music which she performed mainly from memory. It was easy to see that she was having fun. With the absence of competition stress, her violin music communicated pure joy. After playing an encore, the room was alive with shouts, clapping, and a standing ovation. A few of the people, including both of her grandmothers, made their way to the stage where they presented her with flower bouquets.

We look back on that sweet day as one of our happiest memories. In her short life, Bethany had accomplished so much and her future looked to be especially bright. During the reception that followed her performance, several family friends asked us how we had succeeded in raising such a wonderful daughter.

Around the time of her graduation, word got out that she was interested in studying medicine. A family friend surprised us by arranging an unbelievable opportunity for Bethany to work in a university research lab for the summer prior to her departure for college. She focused all her energy into learning as much as she could about the research project to which she was assigned. By the end of the summer she had made a significant contribution. Months later, the research physician bestowed the honor on Bethany of being named the first author on the published research abstract.

Somehow we survived Bethany's senior year, however a nagging uneasiness had settled into our hearts. Each day brought her departure to college a little closer. The joy she emanated during her graduation concert slowly dissipated over the summer and seemed to be replaced by a shadowy anxiety. We attributed all of it to her upcoming transition and assumed it was only normal for each of us to feel anxious.

As her departure date drew nearer, she began to voice regret for not seriously considering the local university associated with the lab where she worked over the summer. The reality of her move clear across the country seemed to be setting in for all of us. We offered her assistance in making arrangements to attend a university closer to our home. After much discussion, she strongly reaffirmed her decision to study on the West Coast. She refused to forfeit such a fine opportunity at the last minute.

Throughout the summer we shopped together to collect the necessary bits and pieces needed to survive in a dorm room and we began to pack her suitcases. A few weeks before leaving Bethany decided to cut her waist-long hair. She donated it to an organization that creates wigs for people with severe medical issues. She updated her wardrobe and looked beautiful. She spoke positively about the new life she was embarking upon but as parents, we sensed a bit of reservation. She was working through her feelings and was clearly positioning herself for transition. The time had come to let her go and see how life would unfold.

FOUR

In August 1999, just like many other parents of college freshmen, my husband and I accompanied Bethany on her initial trip to the new university. We scheduled a flight a few days before student orientation which allowed time together to enjoy tourist attractions and help her acclimate to a new city before classes started. After a long day of traveling she settled into a hotel with us until move-in day. Together we had fun exploring new sights, purchasing a computer and a few last minute items. We wanted to support her throughout the transition, but we also needed reassurance that she had made the right decision and was safe.

Leaving our daughter in a place so far from home was a huge event in our lives. But our concerns were relieved somewhat after sitting through an orientation session reserved exclusively for the highest achievers in the freshman class. The Dean greeted students from all over the world by informing them that they were the "best of the best" and "the cream of the crop." We were proud that Bethany was moving into a dorm reserved for students with the highest academic standing.

"Move-in" day on campus was one of those beautiful late summer days generating a "back-to-school" feeling. Everywhere we looked we saw students and families carrying boxes and colorful belongings into the dorms. It was impressive how friendly the other students appeared, and it seemed obvious that Bethany would easily fit in. We believed she would connect with the students in her dorm and develop friendships.

The campus environment was beautiful, safe, and secure. It looked like a perfect place for Bethany to reach her full potential. We were left feeling a bit awestruck.

Bethany seemed a little nervous, but relieved to be finally settled into her dorm room. The following day we met with her one last time before driving to the airport. At this point we sensed her eagerness to have us depart so she could get on with her life. As we hugged, she assured us that she would be fine and would keep in close touch through phone and email. After parting we paused long enough to watch her walk across campus with her leather backpack slung over one shoulder until she finally blended into a crowd of students.

As her father and I boarded the plane for our departure we felt a rush of mixed emotions. A chapter had ended and a new one had begun. After months of preparation for her transition, it was suddenly all over and we needed time to process our thoughts and feelings. Even though we knew we would miss her it felt as though a weight had been lifted, similar to when she first left home to attend summer violin camp. We wondered if other parents felt relief after dropping their children off at college.

Upon our arrival home, the emptiness of Bethany's room and the absence of her music hit us full force as we realized her childhood was gone forever. I remember walking through her bedroom and considering the things she left behind, the little tokens of childhood memories. I saw my reflection in the row of mirrors above her dresser, where she checked her posture and fingering while practicing her violin, hour after hour each day. In her closet I spotted her bathrobe. I grabbed it, buried my face in it, and wept for all that had been and all I would miss. She had moved on and it was time for her to grow and develop into the woman she was meant to be.

Lingering concerns began to magnify within the first few weeks. We had strongly urged Bethany to allow time to adjust to her new environment before jumping into too many extra scholastic commitments. Also, we had stressed the importance of developing friendships, and emphasized her need for healthy balance between academics and social activities.

She was registered for an ambitious load of classes which included organic chemistry, a subject notorious for being difficult and complex. Due to the university's high academic ranking, we expected her coursework to be quite challenging. We also suspected that, like most college freshmen, it would take her a few months to adjust to the many changes in her life.

Despite our advice, she was like a racehorse out of a gate. Immediately she pursued an opportunity to work in a research lab on campus and was granted a position. Her summer work had given her a large advantage over other students. Later we learned that the position required a special badge to measure radioactivity, which required her to reveal her age. Reportedly, the research professor was very surprised that she was not yet eighteen. Had he known up front, the opportunity may not have been granted.

We were worried she had taken on this responsibility before knowing how much time she would need for her coursework. We also knew the commitment would greatly decrease her free time to connect socially with other students. Little did we know that she had one more surprise to reveal. She auditioned for the University Community Orchestra and was granted the position of concertmaster. It all came too easy for her and it all came too quickly.

Communicating with her became problematic from the very beginning of her college years. Throughout her very busy first semester we communicated with phone and email but it became increasingly difficult to get in touch with her. When she did answer her phone she was always busy and did not talk long. She seemed to limit the information she was willing to share. On the other hand, she did inform us that she had chosen a local church to attend. During our conversations she would briefly mention different acquaintances at school and at church, but spoke little about attending social activities with individuals or groups.

As the semester progressed, she casually mentioned that she usually ate alone in the cafeteria or alone in her room, due to her schedule. Our concern grew. We looked forward to the Christmas break where we could really evaluate how she was doing.

The holidays arrived and it was too expensive to fly her home for both Thanksgiving and Christmas. We wondered what she would do for Thanksgiving as the university food services would be closed the entire weekend. She seemed to care little about connecting with other students remaining in the dorm. Her lack of planning really bothered us. We felt badly about her having no plans for Thanksgiving dinner, but it was her apparent disregard for social connection that concerned us the most.

Bethany flew home after completing her final exams in December 1999. It was amazing how after living through all the emotional details of her move and adjustment, she was suddenly home again. In a way it seemed like she had never left.

Our family entered into our traditional plans for the holidays. Bethany played her violin for the Christmas Eve candlelight service and we hosted our annual New Year's Eve party in our home for close friends. Throughout the break she seemed to relax and we reassured ourselves that she was okay.

When her Christmas break ended, we were unprepared for the emotion of having to part with her for the second time in just a few short months. Our hearts were still a bit raw and it hurt to drop her off at the airport all alone to travel so far away. But she had gained an air of confidence she had not possessed when leaving us back in August.

When she was settled back on campus we spoke to her by phone at least weekly and continued to communicate through email. She never talked long because of her schedule, and her phone calls became less frequent. She said she spent most of her free time in the lab and often worked into the night hours. Just like in the previous summer she was producing a great deal of data.

In the lab, she worked alongside graduate students and research professors. She loved the lab and it seemed to become her main focus. However, we began to pick up on some frustration in her voice when she described different aspects of her work and her interpersonal relationships with a few of the researchers.

Because she held such high academic aspirations and had consistently earned a high grade point average throughout the years, we were confident she had the ability to succeed in her coursework. Our confidence was maintained when she earned very respectable grades in her first year at the university. Self-motivation and achievement had never been a problem for her.

Because hard work is often rewarded, it came as no surprise to us when she was asked to stay on at the university lab over the summer to continue her research project.

In August 2000, and just prior to Bethany's sophomore year, I flew out to spend a few days with her. Throughout the visit we had a great time together. We walked all over the campus, ate in her favorite restaurants, shopped, and talked for hours. She seemed excited about her life and happy in her surroundings. I had the opportunity to see the research lab and her work station which was loaded with stacks of petri dishes and bottles of chemicals. Bethany provided a basic explanation of the project she was working on and introduced me to a few of the researchers. I was very impressed and noticed how comfortable she appeared in such a highly technical environment.

Our days together passed too swiftly and again, just like at Christmas I had to face the emotion of parting with her.

I hold a picture in my mind of her standing all alone on a street corner of the campus perimeter, waving goodbye as the airport shuttle drove me away from her and toward the airport. Despite her accomplishments and aspirations she appeared so small and vulnerable standing all alone. She was so far from home and out of easy reach. No phone conversation or email could ever compare with time spent together.

On the long and lonely flight home, I spent a lot of time thinking about her life. Although she had been a gracious hostess, she had become quite defensive when we discussed the extensive amount of time she spent each day in the lab and how she usually chose to stay alone very late into the night. It bothered me tremendously that she walked back to her off-campus apartment in the dark and all alone. This was clearly a safety concern as well as an issue of social isolation. When I mentioned these concerns she began to debate with me and simply would not yield to recognize the potential danger. She cited very tight campus security and a seemingly safe neighborhood. I was left to comfort myself with the thought that she knew her environment better than I did.

It was disturbing that she did not seem closely connected to anyone on a social level. Beyond her church attendance and daily contact with busy roommates and students in her classes, she did not mention having any close friends. She seemed to be following the pattern she had developed in high school: socially pleasant, academically driven, but very busy and not closely connected to anyone in particular.

August 2000 marked the beginning of Bethany's sophomore year in college and our son's senior year of high school. With our children maturing and striking out on their own, we began to feel it was time to make a move from the Cleveland area and to start a new chapter of life. We hoped to move a little closer to Bethany after our son's graduation from high school. Our son was planning to attend an out-of-state college the following fall, so we had nothing to necessarily keep us in Ohio. Bethany made it clear that it did not matter to her where we lived, as she was established in her new life at the university. When she had spent time with us during her Christmas break, she had not connected with any of her old friends.

Shortly after starting her fall classes in September 2000 Bethany briefly returned home to connect with professionals from the Cleveland research lab where she spent the summer following high school. The research team invited her to join them for a conference in Canada to present and discuss their data. It was great to have her home again, even though our home was just a stopping off point on her trip. She seemed very excited to be included for the presentation of the research project. She appeared vibrant and healthy. We were amazed at the way she was progressing in the field of scientific research at such an early age. After the short trip to Canada, she returned to her university and fall flew by with amazing speed.

Moving in the spring was beginning to look more certain as job opportunities became available for my husband. One thing was becoming clear. Most likely, Christmas 2000 looked to be our last Christmas in the home where our children grew up.

With the arrival of the Christmas season, our beloved fourteen-year-old family dog, Sparky, became severely ill. We made the painful decision to put him down in early December. My husband and I, together with our son, chose not to tell Bethany until she returned home for her Christmas break as we knew she was under a lot of pressure studying for final exams. When arriving home, she was quick to notice his absence because he did not come to greet her. It was difficult having to break the news to her, but she appeared to handle it better than we had expected. Our family adored him and his departure left a gaping hole in our hearts.

Christmas 2000 felt different from previous years because we were processing grief over the loss of our family dog. We also expected the New Year to bring many changes. Each of us realized that as a family, we were nearing the end of a chapter of life. Bethany had lived away from home for eighteen months and our son had only one high school semester to complete before moving to an out-of-state university campus. My husband and I were also approaching a final decision on a geographical move. Because the thought of experiencing Christmas at home without our little dog was so painful, we chose to spend Christmas with our extended family. We returned home in time to host our annual New Year's Eve party.

We noticed that throughout the holiday break Bethany seemed a bit touchy and distant. Instead of readily joining in with family and friends, she seemed to hold herself back. We assumed the loss of our dog had deeply affected her. When we questioned her about it, she said she was fine and explained how her life had developed beyond our home environment. When we heard her softly crying in her room at night she made it abundantly clear that she wanted to be left alone.

In January, as she prepared to depart for the airport, she seemed to brighten up. She was eager to return to her life at the university. Realizing that it would be the last time she would walk through the front door of her childhood home, I grabbed my camera. I snapped a picture of her standing in front of our red front door next to her suitcase. Her violin case was in her hand. It is a poignant treasure, the last portrait from a wonderful chapter.

FIVE

Spring of 2001 brought a period of transition to our family. Our son was preparing to graduate from high school and my husband and I were packing to move from Cleveland to Cincinnati, Ohio. After serving fourteen years in a very fine Cleveland area church, my husband and I felt a tugging at our hearts to make a fresh start in another church. We had hoped to relocate closer to the West Coast, but when the congregation from the Cincinnati church called my husband to be their pastor, it just felt right.

Along with processing an entire life transition, we were dealing with the bittersweet emotions of becoming empty nesters. It was a turbulent and stressful time. We were leaving the home which held everything familiar and secure. We were also leaving friends who loved us and watched our children transition from children into adults. Our family's comfort zone was being uprooted just like an established oak tree. The move to Cincinnati was finalized and scheduled to take place in June 2001.

Against this backdrop of change, new concerns began to emerge in regard to Bethany. Although we continued communicating with her by phone and email, she began to share less and less personal information with us. She allowed us to financially support a significant portion of her tuition and living expenses, but did not allow us to know many details about her life. We did not understand why we she was pushing us away, and assumed she was going through a period of adjustment in becoming an independent adult. We rationalized that a bit of defiance might just be a part of the journey.

Her priorities and goals were clearly changing. When she did share information, she explained that although she was still earning good grades, an exceptionally high grade point average was no longer the most important part of her life plan. We found this starkly different from her former way of thinking and when we questioned her about it she shut us down. She said no one would care about a "B" in a class or two as long as she was able to produce outstanding accomplishments in the lab. Actually, this reasoning made some sense to us. In a way it seemed almost healthy that she was giving herself permission to earn an occasional B in a class. It was her attitude that bothered us, not her logic. It just felt wrong.

On the positive side, she seemed to have established some friendships in her church. Also, right after Christmas break she took advantage of an opportunity to move back into an apartment on the main campus with a new roommate, as she found the walk to and from the off-campus apartment to be too time-consuming. We breathed a sigh of relief, knowing she was back within the safety of the campus perimeter and no longer walking several blocks alone at night after finishing up in the lab. She remained devoted to the work she was doing in the laboratory but increasingly and more openly expressed discontent with portions of her research project and a few relationships with coworkers.

We were becoming disturbed about subtle changes we detected in Bethany's personality. In contrast to the sweet, humble person she had always been, we began to witness a growing arrogance. She was argumentative when we offered any input or guidance about her choices, and increasingly secretive about her activities and plans. It felt like she was becoming resentful toward our involvement in her life.

At the end of June 2001 a large moving van pulled up to our home. During the move, as furniture was taken out of the rooms, we found a little macaroni angel ornament Bethany made in grade school which had fallen behind her dresser. It had a blue satin ribbon and a bow-tie noodle for wings. We also discovered a dog bone which was hidden under a couch. These little tokens called to mind a simpler time. The sweetness of childhood had somehow faded into the turmoil of young adulthood. Together, my husband and I stood in our empty house captured by the shadows of joyful youth which we knew would never come again. Change had arrived and it was painful.

With the completion of our transition, the anxiety we felt about Bethany began to dissipate to some extent as the summer wore on. Throughout our move she showed genuine interest, and offered encouragement. She also said that for her, things were going very well.

In August we traveled with our son to his university and got him settled into his new life. Somehow over a two year period of time, we survived moving both of our children on to college campuses, losing our dog, parting with family friends, leaving the house we all treasured as "home," and starting new jobs. Just about every area of our lives was affected by change. At times, my heart ached to just go "home," to swing open the red front door of our former house to find my young family and our furry little dog inside and eager to greet me. I knew each one of us would have to process change and loss in our own individual way.

As fall of 2001 flew by, most of our communication with Bethany was by email as it became harder and harder to reach her by phone. Once again, anxiety began to weigh upon our hearts. When we did connect by telephone she was pleasant and polite but always pressed for time. If we asked too many questions about her life or offered too much input, the conversations rapidly transitioned into debates. She responded by answering fewer emails and phone calls. She limited the frequency of communication to once or twice each week, which she claimed would be more "typical" for a college junior. In essence, she would be the one to control how much we were allowed to communicate with her.

As she distanced herself from us, she told us she had a new friend who was studying counseling and offering classes on counseling techniques. Bethany had begun attending the classes. We found this quite curious because up to this point she had never shown the slightest interest in any sort of psychological counseling. This was particularly disturbing in combination with the way she regulated all our interactions with her. It was confusing and very difficult to sort out.

In late fall 2001 Bethany called and surprised us with news that she had been given an opportunity to join a team from her church on a ten day mission trip to China. The team would be comprised of students and adult sponsors. She sounded very excited to go. The trip was scheduled right after the Christmas holiday and would cut into her first week of January classes. She planned to communicate with her professors about the lectures she would miss at the start of the semester. Funding was provided mainly by her church, and the trip looked like a good opportunity to serve others while gaining a broader perspective of the world. We found it refreshing to hear Bethany actually excited about something other than her progress in the lab.

In early December, with Christmas preparations on our minds along with Bethany's upcoming trip to China, we received a second phone call from her. She stunned us by asking if she could take one of our cars for a spur-of-the-moment trip to Chicago (about four hundred miles away) all by herself during her Christmas visit to our new home, and prior to her trip to China. She had never actually been to Chicago, other than driving straight through it on a family vacation. Also, to our knowledge she had not driven a car since leaving our home as a high school senior. She said it would be fun to venture out alone and perhaps connect with distant, extended family members. She also wanted to see new sights.

We were dumbfounded by her request and the way she communicated it to us in a cool, nonchalant manner. She expressed no consideration for our feelings, or any plans we might have made for our own family of four. Since we no longer had close family members living in the Chicago area, we knew she would have no place to stay. We also knew she had no extra money to pay for food and gas. To add to the impossibility of her request, we did not have a spare car for her to take. We could not risk giving her one of our cars which we needed for our jobs, and of course it was our employment that generated the funding for not only her college bills, but her brother's college bills as well.

With firmness and a bit of reactive frustration and anger, we turned down her request. She dropped the subject, but we were left with a clear message: she wanted to limit time spent with us during her short Christmas break. Due to our move and getting her brother settled at his college campus, it had been roughly a year since we had seen her. We wondered if she was still dealing with emotions from our move. In coming to see us, she would have to face her first family Christmas away from her childhood home. We expected it would be odd for both of our children to spend the holidays in a strange city and in a house they had never seen before.

It felt awkward preparing for Christmas in a new environment. We set up bedrooms for each of our children with their own furniture in order for them to feel comfortable and welcome in our home. The personal possessions they left behind remained packed in boxes in our garage, as there was no reason to unpack them unless for some reason they decided to move back in with us. Our house would simply not feel like "home" to them and we knew it.

After months of being apart, it was a healing experience to have our family reunited, but we felt tension in relating with Bethany. Although she appeared to be enjoying herself, she seemed uneasy, and emotionally just a few steps apart from us. During one of our family conversations, we casually mentioned the financial stress of having two children in college at the same time. We discussed the eventual need for her and her brother to obtain work in order to contribute to their living expenses and tuition. Although our new home was modest, Bethany responded by suggesting we sell our possessions and move into a smaller house to simplify our lives. We were taken aback at her critical attitude especially in light of how much we had sacrificed to offer her special opportunities in life.

On one day of the Christmas break, when out shopping with her dad, Bethany shared a dream about her childhood that was disturbing her. In the dream she described how I had abused her in some way, so she wanted to find a time to discuss it with me. When her dad heard this he firmly shut her down and told her to keep her dreams to herself. He saw no reason to have me hurt by being dragged through the details of something that was not real. He wondered if the "dream" stuff had something to do with the counseling classes she was taking.

Shortly following the dream conversation, Bethany received a phone call on our home phone which she answered in our kitchen. The call seemed to make her very uncomfortable. Our impression of her side of the conversation was that the friend called to check up on her because several of Bethany's responses included how she was "safe" and "okay." This greatly disturbed us. We could not imagine why she would not be safe with her own family, and we wondered what sort of things she was saying about us to other people. We knew it was possible that the "counselor" was guiding her to believe things that were not true.

The phone call she received, along with her strange request to travel to Chicago, put us on edge and we did not quite know what to make of it all. What we did know was that it felt deeply hurtful. We decided to confront her because it felt like she wanted to limit her time with us. We also wanted to know why she might not be safe in our home and why she apparently believed her dream about abuse had some sort of connection to reality. When confronted, she quickly dismissed and minimized our concerns and seemed to turn her attention to enjoying the holiday. By directly confronting her, it felt like we had sort of "cleared the air" for a new start. As the days passed, she seemed more relaxed and settled as we spent time together as a family. We felt like we were being put through some sort of "testing" period after being apart from her for so long. As we "passed" little tests, she allowed us to draw closer to her emotionally.

Instead of sitting around grieving for the past, together we decided to keep some old traditions and try some new ones. On Christmas Eve, Bethany chose to play her violin for the candlelight service in our new church. On Christmas Day we hosted three international college students from the local university who joined us for a traditional turkey dinner. It was a bit of an adventure to share our culture with them and also learn about holiday customs in China and India. The day after Christmas, Bethany went skiing with her brother and a friend, something she had never done before.

Throughout the Christmas visit, Bethany anticipated her mission trip to China and together we collected the little things she needed for her journey. Each day she seemed to have a great deal of energy and physical endurance, even though we suspected she was not sleeping well at night. We wondered if she stayed awake reading like she often did during her high school years. When we questioned her about it she became touchy and defensive. It was difficult to get a straight answer from her on just about any topic.

Bethany spent some of her boundless energy each day by taking long walks through our neighborhood. She wore a backpack filled with heavy books in order to condition herself for her trip to China. In an odd way, this seemed to be somewhat reasonable. Overall, we were glad she had found friends in her church and hoped the ten day trip would allow her quality time to deepen those relationships.

Surely we were all adjusting to massive change in our family, and each of us needed time to heal. Sometimes we wondered if we were being overly critical of Bethany, as unusual and questionable things seemed to always end up having some sort of logical reason or explanation. It was hard to sort things out and we fell far short of understanding what was motivating her actions.

SIX

In mid-January 2002 Bethany completed her short-term missionary trip to China. Throughout the trip she sent us a few brief informative emails. Her group traveled by bus into remote areas of China, and interacted with many people living in poverty. The experience truly expanded her perspective on the world.

Upon her return to the university she sounded energized and happy when she initially called us, but later mentioned being deeply affected by the desperate poverty she had witnessed. She mentioned a profound emotional connection she had made with many of the Chinese people. The simplicity of their lives made a strong impression upon her.

Bethany had always been a compassionate person with a tender heart. She especially loved people. One Christmas in high school, she used all the money she received as gifts to purchase a goat for a struggling family in a third world country. This was accomplished through a mission organization.

We were relieved to know she was back on campus and once again focusing on school. We understood the importance of the junior year and expected her classes to become progressively more challenging. Naturally, we assumed she would devote an increasing amount of time to her studies.

During one of our phone conversations Bethany shared that a friend was encouraging her to become a medical doctor so she could apply her passion for biology toward fighting infectious disease in Africa. This idea seemed to captivate her. By combining her love for research with a medical degree, she would be specially equipped to help alleviate suffering in the world. She had mentioned this briefly during the Christmas holidays but we viewed the idea as a long-term goal, one that would be realized only after many long and difficult years of schooling and clinical work. Little did we know that she planned to execute a preliminary version of this goal the following summer.

Toward the end of January, Bethany sent a group email to family and friends summarizing her trip to China. In this email she passionately appealed for donations which would fund her on an extended summer trip to Africa, and announced her intention to care for underprivileged people inflicted with AIDS. We were stunned and blindsided by the email. She explained that through a friend, she had established a connection with an African medical missionary who extended an invitation for her to spend the entire summer working at a clinic.

Her plans seemed to have appeared out of thin air and frightened us. We felt panicked, and communicated to her that her plans sounded risky and dangerous. We tried to dissuade her from going, but the more we opposed her, the more firmly she stood in her decision and seemed to draw away from us. We could not understand why she was so strongly driven to plan such a sensational trip right after returning from China. Her passion and rigid determination pressed firmly against the boundaries of our comfort zone.

She was reportedly in close communication with the head physician of an African mission who was apparently very excited to have her join his staff in Kenya. Her plan was to travel alone and live with several young women who were established workers at the clinic. Bethany was very eager to share her own research with the physician and learn as much as she could about the work he was engaged in. She explained that even small laboratories held the potential to make major contributions in the scientific world, and the sharing of data was extremely vital.

As days passed we began to second-guess ourselves and wondered if we were somehow being too critical and shortsighted.

Throughout her young life, Bethany earned a great deal of respect from the people who knew her, as she was known to be sensible and responsible. Her email was a heartfelt, merciful, and self-sacrificing appeal. She shared her summer plans with the congregation at her university church as well as the church in Cleveland where she grew up. With a noble vision, she pleaded with family and friends to help finance her trip.

We were overwhelmed by her incredible plans. We urgently told her how we needed more specific details, like the exact name of the African mission, the physician's contact information, the name of the formal organization which supported the work, and exactly what she would be doing. We held a great concern for her health and safety. Bethany readily agreed to share all this information with us and then proceeded to skillfully dodge our requests. She assured us that we would have everything we needed to feel confident well in advance of her early June departure.

Her plans deeply disturbed us, but at the same time we marveled at our compassionate, motivated daughter. Some young women her age had irresponsible, wild lifestyles. Other young people cared only about themselves. Bethany's desire was to spend her summer in Africa caring for AIDS patients and collecting research data.

A few friends and family members expressed some concern, but overall, people seemed to be favorably impressed by her enormous compassion. We wondered if we were just being reactionary and narrow-minded, but our hearts were troubled. Her timing seemed wrong. Instead of focusing her attention on finishing college, she was suddenly throwing herself into this fearless newfound passion for Africa.

As weeks wore on we became increasingly powerless to stop the momentum she generated toward her departure for Africa. She grew progressively more secretive about the details of her life and we were left on the sidelines holding a huge number of unanswered questions. We were left to wonder and worry.

During conversations with Bethany we carefully guarded the words we chose. Every time we disagreed with her it felt as if a wedge were being driven deeper and deeper into our faltering relationship, and severing it bit by bit.

We recognized and commended her on her compassion, but advised her to suspend all travel until after her graduation. We emphasized that by completing a medical degree or even her bachelor's degree, she would find even greater opportunities in the future. We presented the option of taking a year-long break after her graduation and before starting medical school if she truly felt an urgent need to donate her time toward the care of those with AIDS.

My husband and I tried to suppress the rising panic we felt while interacting with Bethany. As phone conversations turned into debates, she gave us the strong impression that if we thwarted her plans in any way, she would press on despite our objections. While she seemed furiously motivated to minister to the poor, we felt the best course of action would be for her to graduate with her class.

We began to wonder if by implementing her summer plans, she would somehow appease what appeared to be a passionate quest for adventure and refocus her attention on completing her education.

Just prior to the spring semester, and while fine-tuning plans for her Africa trip, she casually mentioned that she was a little burned-out from long hours of studying and attending difficult classes. She decided to give herself a break by taking a few easy elective classes. This would postpone the more challenging coursework until her senior year, after her return from Africa. Even though she was never very artistic, one of the electives Bethany chose was a watercolor painting class. She said the class would relax her.

We also came to understand that an issue between Ohio rules and her university restricted her from transferring all the course credit she earned in community college. Although this deeply bothered her, she assured us her college transcript was in excellent standing, and that the slight diversion in taking a few easy classes would not significantly affect her overall academic plan or graduation date. Even though we readily understood how she could be worn down after so many years of intense study, her timing seemed to be especially poor. We wondered if this "burnout" would threaten everything she had so diligently worked to achieve.

Bethany had become guarded in sharing specific information about her grade point average. We began to suspect that it might have slipped a bit beyond her comfort level. When we questioned her about it, she refused to give us a straight answer. Her evasive answers intensified the growing panic we felt in regard to our general relationship with her and the unusual and seemingly pressured direction her life was taking. We implored her to place her academic standing as a priority over what seemed to be an overwhelming drive to provide relief to a suffering world.

We had never even considered the possibility of Bethany graduating late or somehow not graduating at all, but amid her fascination with Africa, this reality began to creep into our minds. Also, we had recognized that for some reason, our daughter's attitude had foundationally changed, especially in the way she related to us. She had become distant, argumentative, and righteously unbending in her views. She was very guarded and elusive if we asked too many questions about her life. When we mentioned our concerns, she promptly dismissed us and assured us that everything was fine. She was quick to reaffirm her plan not only to complete her bachelor's degree but to continue on and become a doctor. She claimed that medical schools not only considered grades, but also the accomplishments made in the field of research. Additionally, she stated that she had already earned a respectable score on the Medical College Admissions Test.

In diverting her attention from school and embarking upon a trip to Africa, Bethany reasoned that she was making a wise decision in regard to future success in life. Even though we were not experts on knowing how to gain admission into medical schools, we did understand the value of the academic transcript. It was easy to understand how humanitarian efforts could be valued on a resume, but we did not believe those efforts would be more important than an excellent grade point average.

Although we had personally invested a great deal of our money into Bethany's education, she made it clear to us we were not to access her school records. Even though we continued to contribute a significant portion of her tuition and living expenses, she said it would be a violation of her privacy if we accessed her transcript without her consent. She reminded us that our relationship was built on trust.

Her bold plans and secrecy turned our world upside down. When we pressed our opinions or requested specific details about her life she responded with an increasingly hostile attitude. A grinding feeling settled into our guts, and our hearts were weighed down with stress as we watched our relationship with our daughter steadily deteriorate. The more we questioned her, the more she dug in and pulled away by cutting our communication time short. We felt pressured to carefully select just the right words and to express ourselves in ways which would not instantly put her off. Many of the emails we sent to her went unanswered or barely answered with a few dismissive words. She was twenty years old and of legal age. We considered reducing our financial support, but decided that was too risky as she was rapidly approaching her senior year.

Despite her heavy reliance on our money, she continued to drag us into a curious balancing act. We had to step lightly in the amount of concern we voiced as well as any form of resistance we exerted upon her plans. We began to fear that if we made one false move she would cut us out of her life completely. With remarkable speed, we had somehow fallen into a severely dysfunctional relationship with our daughter. We were at a loss to understand exactly how we had failed so miserably as parents. We had become players a in a very high stakes game and life had spun out of control.

Funding for Bethany's Africa trip flooded in from generous people who recognized her selfless passion. When we measured ourselves against the enthusiastic people who eagerly supported her, we began to feel like the only ones who did not value her compassionate heart. Certainly, from all appearances our daughter was an exceptional person. Her desire to care for suffering people instead of relaxing over her summer break was unusual to say the least.

The impact of her written pleas for support bought donations from the most unlikely people, such as friends of people we barely knew. Her plans appeared to be noble, and she was admired. The more she succeeded with fundraising, the more she considered us to be closed-minded. She informed us she was still earning excellent grades and was soon to be named first author on a second research publication. When she reached her financial goal she began to finalize her plans for Africa.

With her Africa itinerary barely completed, Bethany enthusiastically informed us of her intention to take a third mission trip the following winter during her Christmas break. She explained that the idea of this new trip had come to her as a revelation from God, who was calling her to lead a group of seven people into Thailand. This news astounded us. It took our breath away and disturbed us on a very deep level.

When she declared her plans for Thailand, we firmly told her we did not want to hear about an additional trip until she had graduated from college and was financially independent. I told her she needed to keep this new information to herself because it was unreasonable and made her sound unstable. We made it clear to her that she had reached the limit for soliciting funds from friends and family. We explained that we would not continue funding her tuition and living expenses if she planned to continue traveling. We emphatically stated her highest priority should be completing her college degree. She readily agreed and assured us that graduation *was* her top priority.

In late spring 2002, just after our heated discussion about Thailand, Bethany revealed that she had distanced herself from the campus lab in order to prepare for her Africa trip. We were greatly surprised by this. It seemed only natural that she would retain strong connections with the lab and seek a new research project in fall when her classes resumed. It was our understanding that she was relying on lab work to supplement her grade point average on medical school applications.

Bethany was scheduled to depart for Africa just one week after her final exams in May and right after concluding her work in the research lab. The sudden changes in our daughter's life made us feel insecure about her future. It seemed as though she was casually tossing aside the foundational aspects of her life. Nearly everything about her which seemed solid and secure was being shaken and scattered.

SEVEN

At the end of the spring semester, a lease agreement required Bethany to vacate her university apartment. This left her without a place to live during the week prior to her departure for Africa. We made the decision to fly out and spend time with her before her trip, as we felt a pressing need to somehow renew our relationship before she left for the summer. Although we had dragged each other through a mountain of confrontational discussions due to our concerns and opposing views, we were at least still talking. Long distance communication had certainly not been an ideal way to maintain a loving and workable relationship with our daughter.

Bethany welcomed our arrival and planned to stay with us in our hotel room for five days before leaving for Africa. It seemed to be a good arrangement for all of us. It would provide quality time to work on mending the frayed edges of our emotions and our relationship. As we communicated back and forth about travel plans she seemed excited and eager to see us.

We met Bethany on the university campus and she proudly took us on a walking tour of the many places she loved. She had become very knowledgeable about the historical details of her academic community. Although we found it all very interesting, we were especially impressed with how comfortable she had become in the university setting. She led us into the residential building which she had just vacated in the center of the campus, and spoke excitedly about the many friends she had entertained in her apartment. She said the spring semester had been a very happy time because her coursework wasn't too intense and she had been able to interact with many different people.

The main floor of her favorite campus library was a large space tightly packed with individual study desks. She said she spent a great deal of time in that room. Throughout the tour she appeared healthy and vibrant. It was easy to see how much she loved the campus environment. Seeing her in person and interacting with her in such a positive way alleviated some of our concerns. We were becoming reacquainted with her and made a concerted effort to better understand her world from her perspective.

At Bethany's request, we made hotel reservations in a specific residential setting several miles from the university campus. The location of the hotel was an easy walking distance to a small college which Bethany had become familiar with through a few of her friends. All of her belongings were stored for the summer and she retained only those things which she planned to take to Africa. These included two huge suitcases, totally stuffed with clothing, and a violin case which held her less expensive, student violin.

She intended to give away all of the clothing to poor people by the end of the summer, and return home with only her violin. As she explained this to us we began to sense some anxiety about her departure. It seemed as though she were facing the reality of her ambitious plans and the fact that she would be traveling alone. Once again we shared our concerns and said it was not too late to postpone the trip. She emphatically dismissed us and boldly declared she was ready to go.

During the spring, we had worked with Bethany and our medical insurance carrier to assure all suggested vaccinations were complete before her departure. We also obtained medication to protect her from malaria. She seemed grateful to receive the medication. Additionally, in the weeks prior to our visit she gave us a list of unusual items which she required, like a quick-drying towel that could be folded into a tiny case, and special mosquito repellant and netting. We purchased these items for her. In exchange, she had promised to provide us with the specific contact information we had not yet received.

On Sunday she invited us to attend church with her. This allowed us the opportunity to talk with her pastor and many of her friends. We were a bit surprised when she arranged for us to join several of her friends for lunch in a local restaurant. It was obvious she had met some wonderful people. They were polite, friendly, and hard-working students with high aspirations.

We were pleased that Bethany was involved in many facets of the local church ministries. Several people made a special effort to compliment us on having such a compassionate daughter, and a few of them mentioned being surprised that she had arranged the trip all on her own. Our overall impression was that Bethany had gained a large measure of support for her summer plans. In comparison to the positive and forward-thinking way other people seemed to view our daughter, we felt narrow-minded and negative because we had discouraged her from traveling, especially alone, to the African mission.

On Sunday afternoon we took time to outline plans for the remainder of the week. Bethany explained she was working on an important paper that needed to be completed before her departure to Africa, and therefore she required time alone and apart from us. She planned to access a library on the small college campus which was very close to the hotel. We had traveled two thousand miles to spend time with our daughter and ended up walking around the neighborhood looking for things to do while she worked in the college library. She justified her time apart from us by making a commitment to join us on a road trip at the end of the week so together we could explore the desert scenery in the area.

There were several uncomfortable moments during that week, but one scene especially stands out in my memory. The three of us were together in the hotel room when Bethany received a phone call. She turned to us and said it was a private conversation. Then she asked us to step outside onto the tiny balcony and close the sliding glass door while she talked on the phone. My husband and I looked at each other with amazement as we stood outside in the wind. We heard enough of her phone conversation to believe the topic was somewhat confrontational. The longer we stood there the more we felt foolish and gullible.

We were at a loss to know what was really going on with her, but we did know we could not directly confront her. We did not want to risk a total breakdown in our relationship right before she left to spend the entire summer so far from home and beyond our reach. As long as we maintained some remnant of a relationship with her we were still connected. Nevertheless, we were acutely aware that Bethany held ultimate control. We knew at any given moment she could choose to cut us off completely. The high level of emotional stress prevented us from entirely grasping the situation. An undercurrent of restlessness and anxiety made us feel off balance and uneasy.

Bethany kept promising, but she still had not given us her contact information. We were desperate for specific names, addresses, and phone numbers. With this in mind we carefully measured our every word and action, but time was running out. Not only had she insulted us by asking us to step out of the hotel room we were paying for, but she spent most of her waking hours in the college library working on her paper. We were devoting a lot of expense just to be with her, but she limited her time spent with us. It began to feel like she was only interested in a place to stay and meals we provided for her in the local restaurants.

Toward the end of our visit she joined us on a day trip to the desert. I had never actually been in a desert before and was struck with the bleakness of the vast and empty landscape. Hot, dry, unrelenting wind pelted us with grains of sand every time we got out of the car to take a closer look at the landscape. Throughout the day we paused a few times to take pictures and due to the angle of the sun our faces appeared to be cloaked in darkness. In our family album, these pictures reside as harbingers of very dark days which were yet to be lived.

On the last day of the visit, our emotions were raw with anxiety and concern. On our way to the airport to catch the flight home, we dropped Bethany off at a friend's house where she had arranged to stay until embarking upon her trip just a few days later. As we hugged and said our goodbyes we sensed reluctance on her part to have us leave her. After experiencing so much frustration in trying to positively relate to her, it was pitiful that only in the last few minutes of our time together we felt our daughter connect with us in an emotional way.

As we gave her a final hug, realizing we were pressed for time, once again she failed to provide us names and phone numbers we could use to contact her over the summer months. She put us off by explaining that she would send it through email. She assured us we would have the email by the time we arrived home. As we walked away from her, we could not help but notice how small and vulnerable she appeared. I hold a picture in my mind of that moment in time. There she stands, leaning against oversized suitcases, nearly too heavy to lift, with her violin case slung over her shoulder. At that moment we wanted to alleviate all our fear and anxiety by just grabbing her and taking her back to Ohio with us where we knew she would be safe. But that was not an option. She was a legal adult making her own choices with rigid and bold determination.

EIGHT

Bethany's itinerary provided her a twenty-four hour layover in Washington DC where my brother and his family lived. She had arranged to spend one night with them before her flight to Nairobi, Kenya. She informed us in advance that she would connect with us by email upon her arrival in Africa. She also explained that she would have very limited access to the Internet near the area of the impoverished medical clinic.

We felt a great sense of relief when we received our first email from Africa. Bethany confirmed that she had safely arrived and moved into a dorm with several other young women. She had also met with the clinic physician. Her message was brief but reassuring. However, she was thousands of miles away from us and once again she failed to provide any contact information. Our only method of contacting her was through her email address. We were quick to notice that most of the emails we received from her were not personally addressed to us, but rather to an entire group of people who financially supported her trip. It was strange to hear news about our own daughter by being impersonally included in a group email. As days passed, she finally responded personally to an inquiring email I sent to her and I received the following:

"Hi Mom,

I am glad to be in touch again. I have not sent an address because I have no address, only PO boxes associated with people I work with...

Living conditions vary from house to house, and the slums are mud huts, the poorest of the poor. We actually have a shower and a toilet, a huge surprise. We have limited water, though. It is more available in the mornings so I shower then. It is cold here as it is winter, similar to September in Ohio. I love to be with people here, the culture is wonderful. I have not yet seen wildlife beyond the goats and chickens and other animals around where I live."

I was so emotionally overwhelmed by this point that it was hard to fully process the situation. I fervently prayed for her and counted the days until her return.

My husband and I hoped the Africa trip would somehow quench Bethany's thirst for travel. We wondered if living in rough conditions and witnessing extreme needs would refocus her energy toward completing her education. We believed that by obtaining professional credentials she would be better equipped to care for hurting people and better prepared to support herself. With her education complete, she could devote an entire lifetime toward the alleviation of human misery if she so desired. We hoped, upon her return, she would refocus her passion and intelligence into her remaining classes with the same passion she seemed to feel for Africa.

With the belief that Bethany was relatively safe and actively fulfilling her summer plans, somehow we began to settle into our own version of summer. As our anxiety began to subside we allowed our thoughts to focus more broadly on our own demanding jobs and on our son.

Throughout the spring we had not only dealt with Bethany's Africa trip, but we also kept in close contact with our son as he completed the rigorous process of earning a private pilot's license. No one had prepared us for the monumental level of stress we were experiencing by being parents of young adults. We had a daughter in Africa and a son who had become legally qualified to fly airplanes.

A few weeks into the summer, just as our raw and ragged emotions were beginning to calm down, we received a particularly disturbing email from Bethany. She said the opportunity to work closely with the clinic physician was more limited than she had expected it to be. This seemed to greatly disappoint her. She went on to describe how every day she was witnessing extreme suffering in the clinic and the intense human misery was having a profound effect upon her. Also, she had come to realize how very little she had to offer toward helping the unfortunate people.

Along with Bethany's disappointment and frustration, she excitedly reported that she had made the acquaintance of a few special people not directly connected to the clinic, but actively engaged in African humanitarian efforts. She went on to explain that they had expressed interest in her medical research and some ideas she had about fundraising, as there was a continuous need for medical supplies. Bethany decided to assist their efforts in the procurement of funds for supplies. Through these friends she had found a tangible way to help reverse the desolation she witnessed all around her.

After learning about Bethany's plans to procure funding, once again, she blindsided us by disclosing plans to fly to West Africa. She was invited to attend a humanitarian conference. Her sudden decision to travel within the African continent confused us, and it made her appear even more impulsive. With our anxiety soaring, we had greater reason to fear for her safety.

She continued to excitedly share information through group emails but despite her explanations, we could not figure out exactly what she was accomplishing in Kenya or intended to accomplish by flying to West Africa. We were deeply troubled by the group emails. Against this backdrop an official looking letter arrived in our mailbox from the university which was addressed to Bethany. It was quite unexpected to have received even one piece of her mail because she had been so careful in guarding her privacy. Because she was out of the country for the entire summer, we paused and wondered if we should open it.

Because of our constrained ability to directly communicate with Bethany, and not knowing if the contents of the letter were time-sensitive, we went ahead and opened it. Inside the envelope we found a notice of academic probation. It stated that her less than satisfactory grades had placed her at risk for losing her scholarship package. This was the prized scholarship she had worked so hard to earn throughout her high school years. It had been her ticket to attend the university of her choosing. It also represented the major source of her school funding. If she lost the scholarship it would make her tuition unaffordable. There would be no way to pay school bills without incurring a massive amount of debt.

We were horrified. The letter confirmed our suspicions and transformed our fears into reality. We had never before received a letter of this nature, and we never had reason to believe that our daughter would purposely deceive us. What we discovered did not reflect the daughter we raised. In our hands we held evidence that she had fundamentally changed, and it shook us to the core. Although she had significantly lightened her academic load in the spring, she had only been able to produce substandard grades. None of it made sense.

We decided to directly confront Bethany about the probation notice even though we knew it would place us at greater risk of being cut off. We composed an email which explained that, due to her being out of the country, we had opened a piece of her mail. We then informed her that she had been placed on academic probation and explained that we did not have the financial resources to fully fund her tuition. She responded with angry defiance, accusing us of invading her privacy. The violation of her privacy seemed to bother her much more than her academic standing. She dismissed the seriousness of the probation notice and said it would be easy to raise her grade point average as soon as she returned to classes in August. Then she claimed there was nothing more important to her than keeping her scholarship. She said she had already registered for fall classes and was looking forward to graduation.

Our emotions had taken a beating from all the stress she had placed us under. She was obviously living her life right on the edge. Although she so casually dismissed our concerns, too much was going on in her life to allow us any real peace of mind. It was hard to believe it could all culminate in a happy ending. But we had no choice but to somehow trust she would pull things together and still fulfill her dreams.

We continued to receive Bethany's group emails from Africa which portrayed abject poverty and deep suffering that intimidated her. But on the other hand, she described her surroundings in a way that was lofty and flowery. She talked about the wonderful and beautiful African culture, the acceptance she felt by the African people, and how she had grown to love them.

She related how amazing it was to minister to others but did not explain what she was actually doing. She made reference to the area where she was living and described it as a slum. There was also a casual mentioning of dangerous areas she needed to carefully avoid. By all account, she had made positive connections with people and intended to maintain communication with them when returning home. Her hope was to raise financial aid for Africa. During her final few weeks abroad, her emails revealed her concern about readjusting to life in the USA after being surrounded by so much illness and desolation.

As the remaining weeks of her trip slipped away, we were eager for her safe return to the university campus, and hoped we could regain at least a semblance of normal life. We were eager to put the Africa chapter behind us. We wanted to chalk it up to just a difficult stage in our overachieving daughter's life. We were weary of constantly feeling worried and anxious.

Bethany's return trip flight itinerary took her back to the home of my brother and his family. Again she would have about twenty-four hours to visit with them before catching her connecting flight to the university area. In accordance with her plans, she was to travel back to the United States with no personal belongings except for her violin. When my brother picked her up at the airport she was wearing an African dress. Unexpectedly, she returned with one of her large suitcases. The suitcase was tightly packed with handmade rugs which she planned to sell. The rugs would be turned into revenue for the African mission.

Shortly after her arrival at the airport, we received a call from her. She seemed relieved to be back and warmly expressed how much she loved and valued us. She was very energized and excited to share details about her trip, but at the same time conveyed very little specific information about what she had actually accomplished, beyond flying across the continent to attend a conference. We figured she was tired from her long trip and would share more details with us later when she had more time to talk. It was a great relief to have her safely back in the United States and communicating with us in such a positive manner.

A day later, after dropping her off at the airport to catch her flight back to the university, my brother called us. He described how Bethany seemed to be emotionally supercharged, and in his opinion was "headed for a major crash." He said she was dirty when she got off the plane and smelled bad. He had to wash her clothing three times in order to get rid of the odor. He found it especially odd that she had arrived at his home with no other clothing except what she was wearing.

We considered the rough environment Bethany had just left and pitied the people who sat next to her during her flight back to the states. We remembered her mentioning water shortages and how they affected her daily showering schedule. Obviously, her dirty African dress was a piece of the summer she had left behind. By all accounts there had not been a pretty ending to her trip, but at least she was safely home.

My brother's statement that Bethany was headed for a "crash" lined up perfectly with our own creeping apprehensions and fears. But in spite of this, we tucked his warning away in the back of our minds.

NINE

Bethany returned from Africa in late August 2002 just in time to begin her senior year of college. Along with the relief we felt as she settled herself back on campus, we were pleased by the way she seemed to be making an increased effort to communicate with us. During phone conversations she was friendlier and more affectionate than she had been prior to her trip, but was very busy and allowed little time to discuss anything of real importance.

We were eager to know specifics about what she accomplished during the summer. We waited patiently while time after time she put us off by telling us to wait until she compiled a comprehensive Power Point presentation for all her supporters. Friends and family questioned us about her trip but we had little to tell them other than to wait for her presentation. One thing we knew for sure, she was thrilled by the connections she made in Africa and was passionate to raise as much money as she could for the mission. We were simply thankful she was safe and back in school.

Within the first days of her return to the university campus, Bethany told us she left her heart in Africa. She said she had formed a strong connection with the people and was grieving. She mentioned returning someday, perhaps to permanently live in West Africa. We understood it would take time to process all she had seen and experienced, especially as it stood in stark contrast with her life at the university. The disparity between the two worlds seemed to disturb her greatly.

Bethany spent time on the phone with us talking through her feelings. During one of the conversations she once again told us to sell our possessions, give the money to the poor and live simpler lives. We were stung by the audacity and timing of her request as we were currently in the process of working out her school finances for the fall semester. Additionally, we had not yet finalized a repayment plan for her to reimburse us for unexpected plane tickets to West Africa and other charges she made on our credit card which she held for emergency use only. We reminded her of our own commitments to her arrival in Cleveland we heard that she was extending invitations to anyone interested in accompanying her to Thailand.

People from our former church knew Bethany very well. They had watched her grow and develop throughout childhood and adolescence. They were quick to sense that things were not quite right with her and contacted us. She was headstrong and unbending in her opinions. We shared with them our own concerns and described the dysfunctional relationship we had developed with our daughter. We told them we had landed at an impasse over the sale of her violin which was being sacrificed to fund a group trip to Thailand.

During Bethany's visit, people from the church expected to see her Power Point presentation about Africa as many of them had helped finance her trip. She never gave a presentation and did not explain exactly what she accomplished during the summer. Even so, she began soliciting funds for Thailand. This was met with resistance as people needed to see accountability before considering additional contributions.

Bethany was frustrated that church members denied her requests, so she pressed her point with a few people. We were extremely uncomfortable with what she was doing and felt the need to intervene.

We sent Bethany an email which directed her to withdraw her request for funding from our former church members. We believed that as our daughter, she represented our entire family and was being troublesome and divisive. At the same time, a special family friend from the church also sent her an email. He voiced concern for her and suggested she meet with a small group of people from the church to discuss her feelings. We later learned that she deleted both of these emails without reading them.

It was obvious that something was deeply affecting Bethany. She had always been a considerate and reasonable person who sought peace and unity. She had also been extremely responsible, especially in the areas of accountability and finances. Those who knew her were troubled by the choices she was making, her attitude, and the developing discord in our family.

A group of friends arranged a meeting at the home where Bethany was staying and she agreed to attend. The arrangements included connecting her father and me into the meeting through a conference call. At the appointed time we were brought into the meeting. We were grateful for the intervention which was set up by people who knew us well and loved our family. We needed their help because we were at a loss to know just how to proceed with our daughter. We hoped the meeting would mend relationships and restore peace between friends. Although we were hopeful, underneath our hope we felt panic and fear. We were living in a nightmare and desperately needed to wake up.

It was a terribly confusing time and we were in crisis. We could not understand how we had landed in such a situation. We were embarrassed that the strife which had developed between us and our daughter had spread past the confines of our own family and into the lives of our friends. It felt as though we had been walking on eggshells ever since she moved out of our home. Every time we voiced an opinion opposed to hers, she pushed us further away. Although we spent countless hours analyzing conversations and decisions, we were unable to sort it all out.

The meeting was short. Bethany responded to the kindest and most carefully phrased questions with cutting defiance. She expressed offense when people asked her to show accountability for donations that funded her Africa trip, and she offered little information about what she had accomplished. She provided elusive answers while boldly declaring her plan to travel to Thailand.

People who were at the meeting later reported to us that Bethany's affect had been very stiff and stonelike. She had not presented herself as the Bethany they had known and loved. She dominated the conversation and responded to questions with dismissive contempt. A few people mentioned they had been shocked by the disrespectful manner in which Bethany specifically addressed us. We later heard that when she realized no additional funding would be granted, she abruptly ended the meeting and left the room without displaying emotion. She had stunned everyone.

One of the people that attended the meeting was a nurse who had some psychiatric experience. She suggested that Bethany might be "schizophrenic." We were incredulous at this statement and promptly rejected the thought that anyone could even suggest Bethany was mentally ill. She was brilliant and talented. She had been the perfect daughter. Throughout the years she had been passionate toward special interests and tended to throw herself into things, but she had accomplished much in her young life. However, having very minimal psychiatric experience myself, I decided to read about schizophrenia on the Internet.

The bizarre and peculiar symptoms we read about such as delusions, hallucinations, and disturbances of language and communication were too sensational and made us recoil in denial. We simply could not apply them to our daughter.

Instead, we strongly believed that as parents, we held a broader insight into her life. We considered Bethany's behavior to be a manifestation of personality traits compressed and concentrated due to too many long years of self-imposed study. In short, we felt she had burned herself out in her drive to succeed. Besides, we could not fathom how mental illness could possibly inspire compassion. It was not "crazy" to be passionate about helping people. We believed her strong will had intensified with her emerging independence and her experience of witnessing poverty and despair. Or perhaps her behavior was a delayed teenage rebellion.

TEN

On the day following the meeting, Bethany flew back to her university. We sent emails requesting her to call us, as we felt deeply grieved at how the meeting transpired. We told her we loved her and just wanted to talk. Days went by and she did not call. We dialed her number and she did not answer her phone. We sent emails and she did not reply. We were heartsick and our fear was escalating. Somehow we needed to realign our world.

We had come to understand that we held little influence over Bethany's decisions. Even so, we needed some way to put a stop to her plans for Thailand. We decided to use the most powerful tool we had in our possession in order to persuade her. That tool was our significant financial support. We knew it was risky to use it as a bargaining chip but we were desperate. Although we did not want to use our money as a weapon against her, we felt it was our last option. I chose to be the one to present an ultimatum to her as I hoped she would connect with me on an emotional level. She had become hardened and I wanted to find a chink in her armor where she would back away from her plans and turn her full attention toward finishing college.

I made a concerted effort to reach her by phone over a couple of days. I was unrelenting and called her from several different phones so she would not recognize my number. Eventually she answered. I heard surprise in her voice when she realized it was me, but she quickly adjusted and conversed as though nothing unusual had ever happened. She sounded a bit strained, but energetic and upbeat. I could tell she was carefully guarding her words. I reminded her how much we loved her, and then said we had financial issues to discuss. I carefully explained our position and that we could not rationalize sending her our hard-earned money each month while she planned a trip for herself and seven other people with money from the sale of her violin. I reminded her of the years it had taken to find the perfect instrument, and how we had sacrificed to pay for it. I simply stated that our checks would stop unless she cancelled her trip.

I immediately sensed that my direct approach had stunned her. After taking a moment to collect herself, she firmly declared her intention to continue on with her plans. She said she would purchase her plane tickets the following day and our withdrawal of financial support would have no bearing on her trip or her education. With casual but stiff dismissal, she stated that she would have no problem funding the remainder of her education with student loans.

In short, Bethany said it was more important to obey God than to receive our money. She politely thanked me for the support we had already provided and agreed to continue a relationship with us. Underneath her cool demeanor I could feel how strongly our ultimatum had stung her and I began to panic. I urgently tried to appease her by explaining that she was still covered under our medical insurance plan and that she could keep our credit card to use for emergencies. I began to trip over my own words. I told her we still intended to purchase a plane ticket for her so she could spend the Thanksgiving weekend with us, as previously planned. I could feel her anger escalating and then suddenly, without warning, she hung up.

I was shocked, and sat motionless in total silence. I could not believe the conversation had gone so badly and my own daughter had actually hung up on me. Her dad was sitting next to me and had listened to my side of the conversation. He was fully aware that everything had blown up in my face. We sat there defeated, not knowing what to do. Bethany had never in her life behaved toward either of us in such a manner. A moment passed, and as we held each other, I broke down and cried.

Later that day we received a short, curt email from Bethany. She said she had cut up our credit card and was in the process of obtaining student loans. She stated that she could take care of herself, and if we chose to send her anything at all she would only accept birthday and Christmas gifts. In regard to Thanksgiving, she said we would have to let her know if we still wanted her to come. We were left feeling like we had intentionally wounded and abandoned our compassionate daughter. We were hurting. I felt like I had been mean. I felt guilty. And in my mind I began to think of myself as a horrible parent. Although we did not know it at the time, this email turned out to be her final communication with us.

Together we tried to comfort ourselves by remembering how resourceful Bethany had become. In our hearts we embraced a hope that despite everything, she would return to us and we would somehow reestablish a close and loving relationship. We chose to believe that despite a trip to Thailand she would somehow pull things together and graduate. If she managed to travel and complete her education, then maybe she could prove that she was right and we were wrong. Unfortunately, positive thinking did not alleviate the deep fear we felt for her and for her future.

I punished myself for having been the one to deliver the financial ultimatum and carried a self-imposed burden of guilt. I replayed our last conversation over and over again in my mind. Did I choose the wrong words? Was my language too direct and confrontational? Was I too emotional? I wondered how I had so efficiently destroyed the remnants of our fragile relationship with our daughter.

At night despair and guilt kept us awake and drove us to reconsider our decision. We started to believe that we had been too extreme. We decided to send Bethany an email which outlined a revised version of our financial support. We explained that we would be sending a reduced support check each month which would at least cover some of her living expenses. Additionally, we purchased a plane ticket for Thanksgiving and emailed it to her. We received no email reply and could not reach her by phone. We sent her a check enclosed in a greeting card which declared our love and our desire to renew our relationship.

With each passing day feelings of deep dread and panic grew stronger. At times it was hard to even breathe, let alone work or sleep. Our chests felt tight and our hearts actually hurt. The emotional torture hit us hardest in the middle of the night when our world was silent and daytime distractions did not occupy our minds. We would lay there and just think. Then, after a few hours of fitful sleep, we would awaken to the nightmare of reality. It was clear that a second chance was not going to be granted.

In our desperation we decided to call the pastor of Bethany's church. We felt encouraged when we learned that Bethany had sought him for counsel and he was aware of the conflict that severed our relationship. He advised us to give her some space. From experience with his own children, he believed things would settle down if we just backed off for a little while. Her birthday was a few weeks away and we asked if we could send a birthday package to Bethany at that time to the church address. He readily agreed with our request and said he would make sure she received it.

On October 14, 2002, Bethany's twenty-first birthday arrived. It was a day intended for celebration, but instead we were grief-stricken and estranged. This most important landmark in her life would pass by without a warm interchange of loving words or a hopeful sharing of future dreams. The package we had mailed contained a few carefully chosen gifts and a birthday check. We imagined Bethany opening the gifts and reading the warm message in her birthday card. Our minds drifted back in time to the gentle, kind young woman we raised and the memory of her senior violin concert where so many friends complimented us on raising such a fine daughter. Joy had overflowed as we celebrated her young life. From that vantage point, the future had looked so very bright.

Throughout Bethany's childhood I developed a deep love for classical music. Every day the sound of her violin had filled our home. In an effort to comfort myself, I kept my car radio tuned to a fine arts station. One day shortly after her birthday as I drove along with a heavy heart, the J.S. Bach *Air on the G String* began playing. I instantly recognized it as the encore piece for her senior recital. Tears streamed down my face as the sad but beautiful music filled the car. My heart was broken. Beauty had twisted into ugliness. Happiness had flown away.

Weeks passed with no communication from Bethany. The answering machine on her phone was disconnected so we could not leave a message. Support checks we mailed to her remained un-cashed and the box we sent for her birthday returned to us unopened.

Around this time I received a phone call from a professor at the university because he had been unsuccessful in reaching Bethany. He wanted to inform her that a space in one of his very popular classes had become available to her. Since the offer was time sensitive, he explained that he would have to pass it on to someone else unless he could reach Bethany right away. He wanted to know if I had a more current phone number for her. Reluctantly I gave him the only number I had, knowing it was the phone she never answered. I felt ashamed to tell him I had no other way of connecting with her. After the conversation I wondered what kind of mother I had become, being unable to get in touch with my own daughter. I knew it was my fault she no longer answered her phone.

On October 22, 2002, a member of our extended family received an email from Bethany and forwarded it to us. The email looked to be a group mailing sent blindly to our relative's address. It was long and spoke of a "very blessed harvest" of developments for a non-profit organization she was establishing. It introduced several professional people as trustees for the organization. We recognized some of the names, which included a few of her friends as well as people she had mentioned meeting on international trips. The email explained that she would be overseas in Asia between December 19 and January 13 and would spend time in Hong Kong and Thailand. She listed a phone number but said she would be fairly unreachable. The email mentioned that there would be an annual meeting for her non-profit organization and corporate money would fund flights for everyone to a central location for the meeting. In this email she also gave the following information:

"As for board meetings, we anticipate meeting once a year to discuss how to make self-reproducing clinics initiated by us that employ local individuals with the goal of training local people to take over the function in time. I believe I mentioned these ideas to you briefly while in Nigeria. We hope to help train the poor in a few countries to be more enabled to then train others, and also to be available to send finances to start up these efforts."

After reading the email we did not know what to think. On the surface it looked as if Bethany had a large group of reliable people supporting her and taking part in her organization, but we had serious doubts. Through an email from one of her friends we learned that she had become furious with us for speaking with her pastor and sending mail through her church. Because of this we chose to stay on the sidelines and watch for any additional information we might receive. We wondered if somehow she really was establishing some sort of organization in conjunction with resourceful friends. We thought that perhaps we had misunderstood her abilities and vision. However, we knew that balancing a full load of college classes along with extensive travel plans, and the establishment of a non-profit organization seemed dauntingly ambitious, even for Bethany.

As October turned into November we prayed that Bethany would soften enough to communicate with us. We missed her. We hoped her anger would subside enough for her to use the plane ticket we sent for her Thanksgiving break. But in our hearts we knew she would not come. Additionally, it looked as though she would indeed travel to Thailand over Christmas, possibly alone, because we had not heard a word about other people joining her.

Our son was very aware of our painful estrangement and his efforts to communicate with Bethany were also unsuccessful. When she cut us out of her life, she cut him out as well. It had become quite clear that the three of us would celebrate Christmas without her. Because of this, we decided to travel out of state to spend the holiday with our extended family. We were in crisis and needed to be with people who loved us.

Two months had passed since we had sent the birthday package to Bethany at the church address. It was too painful for us to let Christmas pass without sending her at least something. We sent a soft black sweatshirt which we thought would keep her warm during her trip to Thailand. Enclosed in the small package we included yet another check. As soon as we mailed the package to the church address, we discovered that Bethany was reportedly still very angry with us for consulting with her pastor, and had entirely separated herself from her church.

During the Christmas holiday we chose not to discuss the details of our estrangement with extended family members because our emotions were too raw and painful. Instead, we made excuses for Bethany's absence. Even though they could sense something was wrong, they were sensitive and did not press us for additional information. We still believed our situation was only temporary, and with a little more time the estrangement would resolve.

ELEVEN

We headed into January 2003 with renewed hope that Bethany would contact us in some way, but she did not. When February arrived, the Christmas package returned to us unopened.

As time passed, the seriousness of our situation became more apparent. Even though we went to work each day and continued to function socially, just below the surface of every thought, a growing sense of panic lingered. Demanding work schedules were mercifully distracting. But when our minds were not actively engaged, they naturally defaulted to our daughter. At night we continued to wrestle with deep fear and an ever-expanding feeling of dread.

It was hard to fathom how we had become so completely shut out of our daughter's life for such an extended period of time. It was confusing. We had been attentive parents but always promoted her independence. We encouraged her to pursue her hopes and dreams. We had been generous, heavily investing in her special gifts and talents. We had loved her. It was hard to understand how we had failed so miserably.

Over and over again we replayed the events that occurred in the months prior to our estrangement. It seemed as though Bethany had not only caught up with her future plans but was now blindly racing ahead of them. We worried about her finances. We worried about her safety and we wondered how she was managing her class load.

Fortunately, even though Bethany walked away from us and from her church, she still had friends who truly cared about her. During our visits we had met a few of them and surprisingly they sought us out to voice their concern and offer encouragement when they heard about our estrangement. They became our only lifeline to our daughter's life.

These friends were exceptional people and were also worried about her. From them we received a few forwarded emails which Bethany sent to them which included updates about her life. We had to be very cautious in communicating with her friends because each time one of them informed Bethany that they communicated with us in any way, she instantly cut them out of her life. We did not want our estrangement to affect the relationships she still held with people who truly cared about her.

In late January 2003, through one of her friends, we received confirmation of Bethany's completed trip to Thailand. Upon her return to the university she immediately began soliciting funds to aid children in Myanmar with extreme medical needs. While in Thailand, she stayed with a married couple she had previously known from the university area. We were privy to a long email Bethany wrote to them, where she explained the events preceding our estrangement. In an effort to mend our relationship with our daughter, we contacted this couple for their suggestions. We cautioned them not to reveal to Bethany that we had communicated. For several weeks we waited anxiously for a reply but none came. It was uncertain if our email ever reached them.

It was a relief when our previously established lifeline of forwarded emails resumed in February 2003. Bethany emailed an attached document to her friends describing the creation of her non-profit organization. Her stated goal was to collect funding for medical clinics in poor areas of the world and to promote the sharing of medical research data between small and large laboratories around the world. She listed a mailing address for her organization where donations could be sent. The address appeared to be located on the university campus.

Although grateful to have a current mailing address, we did not mail anything to her, as we did not want her to know we had the information. If given enough time to process her feelings, and successfully pursue her compassionate interests, perhaps she would take the initiative of directly contacting us in some way. We did not want to make things worse than they already were.

There was still enough time to make travel arrangements for attending Bethany's graduation ceremony in June. We prayed for an end to the estrangement. In achieving such a major accomplishment in her life we were certain she would want to have us attend, if for no other reason than to prove that she finished college without our help.

My husband expressed his doubts about her even graduating at all. I was clinging to hope.

In March 2003 we unexpectedly received a letter addressed to us from the university. It was a notice informing us that Bethany had abruptly moved out of her university housing. From what we could gather, it appeared as though she dropped out of school as well. The letter devastated us.

Without delay my husband contacted the university. Details were sketchy. No one had anticipated her departure. She simply turned in her key and walked away. He tried to get answers from some of her friends and a few people listed as board members for her non- profit organization. One of the members claimed to not even know her. No one at the university, none of the friends we knew, and none of the people we had been able to contact from her organization could tell us anything. She was gone.

Despite our panic we somehow accessed her online transcript and discovered she had received failing grades in all of her fall classes. Our daughter, with all her high aspirations and outstanding accomplishments, had flunked out of college. It was unthinkable, but the official transcript lay before us as proof. No longer was there a need to wonder how she managed a full-time senior class load while traveling and establishing a non-profit organization. We had our answer. She was not managing at all. Her life had fallen apart.

Despair gave way to guilt and I began to believe that her failing grades were entirely my fault. I was the one who delivered the financial ultimatum. I was the one she hung up on. Despite her urgency to travel, I could not help but contemplate whether she would have remained in college if we had only continued to send our full financial support. Maybe we had placed too much stress on her. I began to question everything and especially our objectivity and ability to fully appreciate her compassionate and intense desire to help the poor.

It felt like there was nowhere to turn and no one to help us. Bethany was a legal adult with every right to drop out of college in order to develop a benevolent non-profit organization. There was nothing we could do about any of it.

We considered other families where daughters and sons had rejected their parents as part of a quest to discover themselves, only to return later after realizing what they had lost. People called them prodigals, and prodigals were expected to someday return.

TWELVE

In March 2003, right after receiving the notice from the university, we learned that Bethany flew to Boston on a short trip. She also had a desire to visit Saudi Arabia. We did not quite know what to make of the news, but it looked as though she was obviously getting money from somewhere to fund her travel expenses. It was possible her non-profit was receiving significant donations and she was in some way generating personal income.

In early April 2003, we received, from the same friend, a cluster of forwarded email correspondences between Bethany and her. The emails were written between February 2003 and April 6th. This friend voiced her concern about Bethany's sense of reality.

In a February 18th email, Bethany was offering to give away her less expensive student violin along with her viola to someone who would use or sell the instruments. She said if they chose to sell, they could keep the money if they wished. She was especially dismissive of the student violin, claiming it would not sell for much money. She wanted someone to enjoy the instruments, as they sat on her desk without being used. She was also offering to give away her valuable collection of violin music which had been an integral part of her life for many years. In this same email, Bethany stated her intention to sell her expensive, lifetime violin.

In a group email from March 10, 2003, Bethany sent out a plea to friends requesting prayer for her non-profit organization as she felt a bit "stalled on the cutting edge," and "waiting for speed in design" in regard to the organization's website. She was also awaiting an "official letter of tax exemption." She mentioned how she wanted to spend her time wisely while waiting for those things to be accomplished.

On April 6, 2003, Bethany sent a long email to a large group of people. She described how she was experiencing an "exciting and exhilarating" time in her life and that her non-profit organization had just been granted tax-exempt status from the Internal Revenue Service.

She was "thrilled" at having earned this status in "record time," and planned to solicit grants from large corporations.

Her email went on to explain how she considered herself to be a missionary to Nairobi and Myanmar. She claimed this status by being a fundraiser for needy people in both countries. She projected her fundraising would bring in "tens of thousands" of dollars. But she also communicated concern, as she said there was no provision in the grant guidelines that allowed monies to be used for her own personal living expenses. Because of this, she extended a passionate plea for personal support and said she was able to live on a "super low budget."

Right after sending this April 6, group email, Bethany sent several additional emails to her close friends. In one of these she urgently requested an invitation to have dinner and spend the night at the friend's apartment. She said she wanted to "rejoice in the new tax-exempt status and sleep." In a subsequent email exchange regarding when and where to meet, Bethany mentioned she was no longer attending her church because a few of the people were "saying bad things about her," and "nobody emailed her." She concluded this email by warning her friend not to bring a third person to the place where they intended to meet.

The emails disturbed us greatly and we felt afraid for our daughter. With a renewed sense of urgency we tried to think of a gentle and non-threatening way to encourage her to resolve our estrangement. During a phone conversation with Bethany's close friend, we asked if she would encourage her to write an article or poem using the theme of "olive branches," because they symbolized reconciliation. We had been waiting for an opportunity where Bethany might feel the desire to contact us, if for no other reason than to request money.

Since we had the address of the non-profit, we decided to send a short impersonal note written not to Bethany, but to her organization. We formally pledged two hundred dollars per month toward staff living expenses and enclosed our first support check. We believed that by sending funds to the organization, we could show Bethany that we still supported her. In return, we expected to receive at least a receipt or some other kind of impersonal acknowledgement. We received nothing in response to our donation and the check was never cashed. Even though Bethany seemed to be in need, she obviously did not want our money.

At the end of April 2003, a family friend forwarded an email from Bethany because she felt concerned about her. The email included a lengthy and detailed introduction and description of her non-profit organization. Her stated mission was to serve poverty-stricken people throughout the world by creating a "bridge" which would connect the educated wealthy to the poorest of the poor. There was also a list of the organization's board members from various countries all over the world.

Along with the informational material, Bethany had included a section for poetry to help illustrate the philosophy of the organization. In this section we found the following poem:

Africa
By Bethany

How unworthy are we
To produce fruit for you
Purple mountains linger under countless stars;
Rainbows overshadow mighty rivers.
Your love is great.

Our consumption of your gifts
Causes seeds to sprout
Healing fruit, filled with water
Of your beauty, tastes of your provision
You make good things.

Olive branches grow strong
We recognize the emptiness inside ourselves
Perplexed by your awesome beauty
Orange skies massive sun gives but a glimpse of you.

Under the poem was a statement that mentioned how "Thoreau's isolation" was similar to the organization's philosophy.

We found it strange that the concept of isolation could be used to bring people together for a cause.

Bethany also included her personal biography and referred to herself as both founding president and administrator of the organization. She mentioned her fascination with scientific study and her lifelong search for something deeper. She listed her most reputable research publication and chronicled her trip to Africa. She described how she suffered through an inescapable water shortage in a Nairobi slum. She claimed to be in her mid-twenties although we knew she was six months away from turning twenty-two. The email concluded by soliciting donations for her organization. Bethany's concept of an olive branch had indeed been stated but we could not understand it.

Around this time we unexpectedly received an email from a young man we did not know. Through the Internet he had searched for, and found "Bethany's parents." His email detailed how Bethany had moved into his female friend's apartment, which was located on the university campus. Bethany had apparently made claims about being a published scientist. He believed she was lying, as she appeared to be "disheveled" and her demeanor did not seem to match the academic claims she had made. In short, he did not feel comfortable having her stay with his friend. We assured him that she was indeed telling the truth, and we encouraged him to access her publications on the Internet. We told him that Bethany was going through a rough time, but she did not pose a danger to his friend. We later learned that shortly after communicating with us, Bethany was asked to leave.

Before receiving the February and April emails, we assumed Bethany received quite a bit of money from the sale of her lifetime violin. We also remembered her statement about applying for student loans during the previous October. Throughout her life she had always been very conservative with personal spending and she knew how to live on a budget. It concerned us that she seemed to be living with friends. The revenue from her violin along with money from the student loans could have supported her for many months. It was difficult to sort out just where she stood with resources, especially in consideration of the trips she made and in light of her refusal to cash the checks we sent to her organization.

After receiving the forwarded emails and the email from the young man, communication came to a standstill. We were left with only random fragments of information we found on her website. It was routine for us to be awakened by panic in the middle of the night. We would then stay awake wondering where our daughter was. Although we were very grateful to have received the forwarded emails, they gave us a feeling of impending doom and left us feeling frustrated, alienated, and guilty.

We had no other option but to wait and let time pass. Our bodies were worn down from lack of sleep. Despite our indescribable situation we had to function responsibly in our jobs. People who knew us had no idea how intensely we suffered. We became very skillful in politely steering conversation away from the well-intended, normal inquiries people routinely made about our family.

We decided not to disclose too many disturbing details about Bethany to her brother. We did not wish to transfer our emotional anguish into the more normal relationship we held with him. Losing one child was bad enough. Also, we did not want him to think too badly about his sister, or to put him into a position where he was required to take sides. He deserved to have emotionally healthy parents who held an interest in his own unique life. Somehow we had to stay strong so grief and despair would not overtake every aspect of our lives.

In early June 2003, we suffered through the weekend that had been highlighted on our calendar for Bethany's college graduation. We had expected the event to be a celebration of Bethany's life and ours, but instead we grieved and imagined her alone, and possibly witnessing joyful families gathering all over the university campus.

In early July 2003, since it had been quite a while since receiving any new emails about Bethany, we sent a few inquiries out to people she might have contacted. One of her trusted friends, whom we knew to be a solid and stable individual, sent us a short reply. This person assured us that he maintained regular contact with Bethany and that she seemed to be doing quite well. He said although Bethany felt the need to be distant from her family, "marvelous things" were happening in her life. He advised us to "give her space," and in time, believed our relationship would be restored and we would come to understand the purpose for the estrangement.

It was a tremendous relief to hear Bethany was actively confiding in a friend, and that "marvelous things" were happening in her life. It was a small glimmer of hope which held a wealth of promise for the future. This information was the only good news we had received in a very long time. We encouraged ourselves with the belief that if we could just patiently persevere, things would improve. We looked forward to a time when we would no longer live in fear and guilt, and our family would finally heal.

A few days later in July 2003 we received a copy of an email Bethany sent to a professional friend. It described a "journal" which was soon to be published by her non-profit organization. In the email Bethany described the journal as a collection of "goldmine" research studies from remote areas of the world. The journal would be delivered to subscribers through the Internet. The email actively solicited research submissions for the journal. When she spoke of her organization, she always used the word "we," which implied several people working together. We did not know if working with a team of people to create the journal was one of the "marvelous things" happening in her life.

In early October 2003 we received a forwarded email Bethany wrote to another professional friend. In this email she mentioned her fascination with some HIV studies she had encountered in Africa, but said her main focus was cancer research. She referred to enjoying healthy relationships with quite a few scientists who were encouraging her to complete her education. She explained that she had recently gone through some major trials over the past year with her parents who were experiencing "extremely severe and confidential marriage problems," so her education had been "slowed down."

The existence of "extremely severe and confidential marriage problems" was news to us. We carried a load of stress and anxiety each day, and knew that, given the circumstances of the estrangement, it would not be unusual to develop marriage problems or even become divorced. However, that was simply not the case. Throughout our marriage we had never encountered serious relationship issues. Generally, any disagreements we had with each other were kept between the two of us for private resolution. Our home had been peaceful and our marriage was strong. It seemed as though Bethany was creating this story as an excuse for not graduating from college. In doing this she assigned us the role of unstable, destructive parents and her role was the innocent victim.

We soon discovered that she had broadcasted this information to several of our friends. Clearly it was a pointed attempt to hurt us and publically discredit us as well. We had never known Bethany to act in such a deceitful and revengeful manner. She had always been respectful, loving and honest. She was behaving in a way which was completely foreign to the daughter we had known and it cut us very deeply.

THIRTEEN

October 2003 marked the one-year anniversary of our estrangement from Bethany as well as her twenty-second birthday. The passage of so much time without resolution amplified our feelings of fear and panic. In an entire year we had accomplished nothing. And actually, our situation had become worse.

When family and friends inquired about Bethany we felt uncomfortable and guilty. Other parents our age were involved in their children's lives at least to some extent as they watched them develop into mature adults. We were not even sure where our daughter was. It was painful not to know how she supported herself and where she lived. It seemed as though only irresponsible and uncaring parents would find themselves in a position such as ours. We began to feel like we should be doing something more than just waiting around for things to improve.

We were deeply concerned about Bethany's welfare. It had been a year and a half since we had actually laid eyes on her, and some of the forwarded emails from spring and summer continued to haunt us. The email we had received which questioned Bethany's sense of reality was especially concerning. We wondered if she had taken on too much and needed a dignified way of backing out of her ambitious plans. We thought about building a sort of bridge that she could walk across with dignity, a bridge that would lead her back into our family.

We called to mind human interest stories where parents went searching for sons and daughters and actually "rescued" them from extreme circumstances. It was easy to imagine all sorts of horrifying scenarios. Anxiety and fear intensified with each passing day. It was time to do something. Against the advice we had received just a few months previously about giving her space, we started planning a trip. If we could somehow find her, we could humbly apologize for opposing her compassionate plans and cutting off her college funding.

The only direct contact information we had for our daughter was the mailing address for her organization. Although we did not know where she was living, we assumed it was near the address of her organization. I remembered that before she left for Africa, Bethany mentioned storing her belongings in a room owned by an older woman. I wondered if she lived with the woman and helped her out in some way.

It was our understanding that Bethany frequented campus libraries and one library in particular. But due to thousands of students on and around the university campus, it would be nearly impossible to randomly run into her. The task would be emotionally and physically daunting. If we did find her, we had no way to know how she would react. After considering all the factors, we decided her dad would travel to the university alone in order to find her and make amends. I would stay home in order to spend time in prayer, pleading with God to help us. It was our hope that once she actually saw her dad, the hard emotional shell she had built around herself would begin to crack. Perhaps she would realize we loved her enough to come looking for her.

Her dad made the long trip to the university in November 2003. On his first day he arranged to meet one of Bethany's close friends who had sent us most of the forwarded emails. The two of them met in a restaurant near the university and talked for about an hour, sharing their mutual concern for Bethany. It was remarkable to comprehend the dedication and compassion this friend held for her.

After the restaurant meeting, my husband went directly to the address Bethany listed for her non-profit. Unfortunately, the address turned out to be a post office box, not a residence. The private establishment which housed and maintained the mailboxes was located just beyond the perimeter of the campus. Surprisingly, the attendant knew Bethany and informed my husband that she usually did not collect her mail on a daily basis. After hearing this, he found a bench near the building and decided to just wait in case it happened to be the day she did collect her mail. The mailbox establishment was situated in a crowded area full of restaurants and shops, frequented by university students. Amidst the rush of people, he could not help but notice a surprising number of individuals who appeared homeless and mentally ill. Many of the food court restaurants set out free food for them. He spent the entire day waiting but Bethany never appeared.

His second day was spent on the university campus. Long hours of walking among the huge crowd of students provided more than enough time to analyze the difficult situation he was in. His return to the university rekindled memories from the week in August 1999 when we moved Bethany into her freshman dorm. The passage of time had brought us so far away from that bright beginning. After searching inside the library Bethany was known to frequent and not finding her there, he made the decision to sit on a bench just outside the library's main entrance and wait. Every few minutes hundreds of students filed past him, headed to their many destinations.

As I waited at home, my husband periodically called to report what was happening. When I heard he was waiting by the library, I became overwhelmingly anxious. I paced the floor and prayed. The hours passed slowly, and suddenly against all odds, Bethany walked right past him.

As she went by, he noticed she was wearing nice clothing and carried a backpack. He was relieved to see her looking healthy and well dressed. He got up from the bench, walked briskly to catch up with her, and called her name from a few steps behind. She stopped and turned with a smile of anticipation, apparently expecting a positive encounter with a friend. When she saw it was her dad, her expression immediately changed into a look of surprise and then into intense anger. Without saying a word, she spun around and walked away from him as rapidly as she could, disappearing into the fast moving crowd of students. He was stung by her dramatic response and did not try to follow her. Although it deeply hurt him to be so decisively rejected, he was thankful to have at least seen her.

Right after the encounter my husband called me. When he told me that he had just seen her, a sudden feeling of joy ran through me like a lightning bolt. But the joyful sensation rapidly dissipated when I heard how angry she had become and how she had turned and walked away from him. Together we took some comfort in knowing that she did not appear unkempt or sick. However at the time we did not know our situation was about to become much worse.

A few hours later, Bethany sent us an email which she copied to several of our friends. It was the first communication of any kind we had received from her in well over a year. With hurtful words she accused us of mistreating her during childhood. She said she would take legal action against us if we ever tried to see or contact her again. Her nasty accusation shocked and humiliated us. We were profoundly injured. By using a few false and powerful words, Bethany constructed a solid barrier around herself which we could not cross.

With a heavy heart, Bethany's dad travelled back to Ohio. When he walked through the door of our home we fell into each other's arms and wept. We were in shock from the encounter and the accusations. We did not know how to even begin processing all that had transpired so quickly.

We no longer knew our daughter. Our Bethany would never have made up such a spiteful accusation. Throughout her life we had treasured and protected her in countless ways. We could not imagine how she could lay such a charge at our feet, and before our closest friends. By so powerfully repelling our attempts toward reconciliation, she had placed us in a position where we could no longer help her.

Although we did not believe she would actually sue us for false accusations, we did not want to further inflame our relationship. If sometime in the future, there was ever to be reconciliation, we now fully realized that Bethany would have to be the one to take the first step. There was nothing more for us to do but pray and trust in God's protection as she continued her journey alone.

We made a few small efforts to dispel the accusations made against us but realized the email recipients were friends who had known us for many years. They would see the truth and draw their own conclusions from what they already knew about our family. Up to this point we tried to keep the details of our estrangement very close, hoping things would quietly resolve and our family's privacy would be preserved. But due to the nature of the accusations and not knowing what would happen next, we felt an obligation to share our painful situation on a wider scale with the people in our church.

In November 2003 our church held a semi-annual business meeting. These meetings were attended by a relatively small group of the most dedicated and long-term church members. It was during this meeting we chose to share our family troubles. We succinctly explained our concerns about our daughter and the serious nature of our estrangement. In an overwhelming demonstration of love, they embraced us and prayed for our family. We cried together while grieving the loss of the gentle and kind young woman who had used her violin to touch so many lives.

We entered the 2003 Christmas season and once again our son joined us as we traveled to spend the holiday with extended family. It was too painful to remain in our home without Bethany. Since so many family members were able to gather together that year, a professional photographer was hired to take an extended family portrait. It was the first and only time we ever did this. Every family member was in attendance except our daughter. Bethany's absence was acutely felt, but our loved ones were sensitive to our feelings and we all carried on as usual. They knew that asking questions about her would only intensify our pain. The one missing face in our family portrait is silent authentication of a very painful estrangement and a dark time in our lives.

The days spent together with extended family during that Christmas season were a healing balm. At times we were surprised to find ourselves actually laughing. It had been a very long time since we had experienced any level of true happiness. During quiet times throughout the holiday season, and in quick moments of reflection, our minds returned to Bethany and the sorrow we felt for her and for ourselves.

We could not help but wonder where our daughter was and how she was spending her Christmas. All that had transpired in the fall shut down any further action on our part toward reconciliation. In an odd way this gave us a sense of release. The road to Bethany was simply closed. We felt it was time to wait and trust that somehow she would resolve her anger and return to us. We had solidly defaulted into this waiting period with no guarantee it would ever end. Somehow we had to find a way to recover at least a small measure of daily joy.

FOURTEEN

As we drifted into January 2004, we began the painful process of redefining our lives while adjusting to a total separation from our daughter. We were still sifting through raw emotions generated by the brief encounter between Bethany and her dad at the university in November 2003. Her use of lies and slander had inflicted a deep hurt upon us and had stirred within us a reactive, frustrated anger due to the injustice of her claims. Our love for her was not diminished but we clearly needed time apart from her in order to heal. It was hard to imagine how such rigid estrangement could ever progress into any sort of resolution.

It was during this difficult time I so distinctly remember a specific evening while driving my car home from somewhere. I had tears running down my cheeks while deep in thought about Bethany's life. I was afraid for her and missed her. As I approached a left-hand turn into our neighborhood, the following question unexpectedly popped into my mind: "Are you willing to wait as long as it takes for *her* good?" With a sense of purpose and renewed hope I answered out loud with a firm, "*Yes*, I am willing to wait." This experience marked a turning point in my journey. I had suddenly been given purpose and the resolve I so desperately needed to reaffirm in my heart and mind that *yes*, there was a master plan and nothing in our lives would be wasted. I knew God was still in control.

After sharing our hearts with the people of our church in November, we carried with us a sense of support. By revealing our pain we had taken a small step out of the shadows where we had been isolated for far too long. The love and support of friends helped to fortify us and give us hope. We had been beaten down for so long and had channeled so much energy into "damage control" in Bethany's life, there had been little energy left for anything else. We had remained committed to our demanding full-time jobs, but most of our "free time" had been spent managing our ongoing nightmare. Out of absolute necessity we made plans for a restful vacation which we intended to take in mid-March 2004.

Even though we felt deeply wounded by Bethany severing her relationship with us, there was no way to escape a feeling of pressing concern for her life. We had an emotional need to keep track of her in some small way. The Internet provided an observation window through public postings on her non-profit organization's website. Throughout February 2004 she was actively posting new material. This allowed us to glean little bits and pieces and paste them together to create an impression and make an educated guess on how her life was progressing.

In one of her website statements, she identified herself as a DNA biochemist and specifically named top-notch medical schools where she had applied to become a doctor. She went on to explain how she had withdrawn those applications in order to shift her focus toward creating an international organization. She described how while in Nairobi, she had dressed and acted like a "slum girl" and experienced "the joy, heartaches and challenges of daily life." She stated her dream of breaking down "barriers between people groups," and said she enjoyed visiting soup kitchens in her city which provided food for the homeless. She mentioned "real-life homeless friends" and how they were mentally disabled and truly incapable of working. She described how they lived on the streets for decades, unable to handle their disability. She loved becoming "all things to all people," and mentioned her vision to help "renovate a city" with huge chunks of money spent on massive clinical expansion in parts of Africa. By moving in two socioeconomic directions at once, she planned to create a bridge between rich and poor. To the uninitiated, her words were powerfully persuasive.

An additional entry from February 2004 described how her organization held a network of staff support which numbered over fifty people in seventeen countries, with most of the countries containing a "third world" population. She announced that her organization had begun sponsoring medical work in a Nairobi, Thailand, and Myanmar, which were places she had personally visited. This work was possible because of a two thousand dollar donation received from a corporate sponsor. She listed October 2002 as the date her organization had become incorporated, and March 2003 when it had been granted tax-exempt status. We wondered how a two thousand dollar donation could fund such ambitious claims.

In a third February 2004 entry she boasted of her organization's desire to support poor people in dangerous and corrupt countries. It was difficult to digest all we read on her website as the scope of information was sensational and diverse. We were haunted by her strong drive to become involved in dangerous and unstable areas of the world. The material we read on the Internet greatly expanded the fear we already held for her personal safety.

No further emails from Bethany's closest friend had been forwarded to us since November 2003, and in early March 2004 we sent her an inquiring email. We wondered if she had moved away from the university area in pursuit of career goals. Our email explained how our estrangement had intensified after my husband's encounter with Bethany in November 2003, and that we had refrained from initiating any communication with her since that time. We were eager to know if Bethany was still living in the university area and if she seemed "okay."

Relief swept over us when we received a forwarded email Bethany had written to her friend describing that she was doing "better," had money, and had purchased a cell phone. In Bethany's email, she suggested getting together with her friend but mentioned her hesitation to meet, as she was unsure if she could "trust" her friend. She kept her newly acquired cell phone number a secret, even from this long-time trustworthy friend. We were grateful to know Bethany apparently had enough money for personal needs and a cell phone. With this reassurance we were able to focus on our much needed vacation. Our bodies were worn out and our emotional reserves were empty from maintaining a constant vigil.

A few days into our vacation we experienced a level of rest and peace we had not known for years. By removing ourselves from familiar surroundings and the stress of our everyday lives, we felt the full weight of our exhaustion. Our time away provided enough refreshment to steer us toward a path of healing, and with a renewed sense of calm we headed home. Strangely, our flight was re-routed during the night and we flew directly over the metropolitan area where Bethany lived. As expansive city lights appeared below us, our hearts relationship we had with him stood in stark contrast to the distorted and grievous relationship we held with Bethany. The unrelenting emotional trauma of her decline had severely worn us down. It also warped our thought process. We had come to think of ourselves as deficient and unsuitable parents. Relating with our son made us feel normal again.

As the summer progressed, basic information about Bethany's life grew increasingly scarce. We wondered if given enough time to succeed in her pursuits, she might return to us even if only to flaunt her success in spite of our withdrawal of financial support. In my imagination I repeatedly played out a scene where one day our doorbell would ring and I would open the door to find her standing right before me, ready to reconcile our differences and reenter our lives. She had fully demonstrated her ability to travel around the world, so it would be easy for her to find her way to our home. I even wondered if she would meet someone from another country, get married and turn up on our doorstep with a child. Anything seemed possible.

One day out of the blue, we received a call from one of Bethany's friends we had never met. This person relayed third-hand information about Bethany's need to have some dental work done and how she had no money to pay a dentist. We offered to fully fund her treatment, but we were never given information on where to send our money or what specific problem she was experiencing. We were left to worry and wonder whether she had accessed treatment or if she had walked away without resolving her problem. It hurt us to imagine her living with physical pain. The third-hand plea for assistance raised broader concerns about Bethany's financial status, and this reinforced our concern about her most basic provisions for daily living.

With the arrival of fall both my husband and I were sleep deprived. We were desperate to take a few vacation days. We decided to hide away in a state park resort in the Appalachian Mountains. It was one of our favorite places as it brought us close to nature and held countless memories of family vacations during our children's school years. On our first evening we settled into an isolated cabin in the woods. Fog rolled in at dusk, blanketing the entire area in heavy darkness. It gave a feeling of being tucked away and hidden from the rest of the world. We crawled into bed and did not wake up until fourteen hours later.

Our lives were continually weighed down by fatigue. Fitful sleep was plagued by real and imagined fears. Nights were long and torturous. But lying awake at night was the worst because it allowed our minds to intensely feel the starkness of reality. Tormented by day and haunted by night, we felt powerless to help our daughter without pushing her further away. There were times in the wee hours of the morning, I would find myself lying face down on our living room carpet, cold and alone, bitterly weeping and silently crying out to God. Together and individually we suffered, each of us in our own way, but we remained sensitive and careful not to pull each other deeper into despair.

October 2004 marked the two-year anniversary of our complete estrangement with Bethany. We missed celebrating three of her birthdays and were approaching the third Christmas without her. On November 4, 2004 I made my first entry into a black leather journal I purchased to help work through my thoughts and feelings.

In addition to journaling, I had a hunger for quality literature which would minister to my wounded heart and open my eyes to the deep truths I longed to learn from our trial. As I devoured literature, I copied favorite verses and passages into my journal and found comfort by reading them over and over again. I dated each entry and often returned to the first page, reading through all the entries in sequence to better understand the progression of our journey. I was able to see how there was a healing force in attendance amidst the trial. My focus was to wait on God for as long as it took for *her* good.

Here is one of my early journal entries:

"You can make many plans, but the LORD's purpose will prevail."
Proverbs 19:21

We began to realize that we were finally transitioning out of a "reacting" mode and into a period of waiting. The tapestry of our lives continued to be woven each day, but Bethany's distinct thread color was no longer a vibrant part of the cloth. Her estrangement had altered the beautiful design we had anticipated for our lives and we had no way to change the pattern. We simply had to wait.

With the arrival of January 2005, the experience of celebrating yet another Christmas as a "family of three" was behind us. We pressed onward and threw ourselves into our jobs. During our free time we found projects to keep us busy. Bethany's dad threw himself into involved renovations on different areas of our house. I began reformatting the many volumes of picture albums I kept which visually chronicled the childhood years of our children. Viewing so many photographs in succession refreshed memories of happy times. I also was compelled to sort through my cedar chest in an effort to somehow build an emotional bridge between the past and the present.

Shortly after Bethany dropped out of college in March 2003 we began receiving default notices on her student loans. They arrived in a slow, steady trickle. During her time at the university, the combination of her scholarship and our monthly support did not fully cover all her expenses. To fill the deficit, she had taken out a few very small student loans which she could have easily repaid once she graduated and started a career. We knew the approximate amount of money she would have needed to borrow in order to complete her degree after our estrangement. The owed amounts on the notices were far beyond what we had anticipated. We did not know if she had taken additional loans without our knowledge prior to our estrangement, or if she borrowed extra money to cover travel expenses.

We had forwarded the first few loan repayment notices to Bethany at her organization's address so she would have awareness of her indebtedness, but the envelopes appeared back in our mailbox unopened and marked "return to sender" by the post office. As additional new notices continued to arrive at our home, we decided to stop opening them and put them aside to be dealt with by Bethany at a later date. We did not cosign on loans for our children as we had made it clear to both of them that earning supplemental income vs. borrowing money was their decision and responsibility. If Bethany desired our assistance in establishing a repayment plan, then we felt she would first need to repair her relationship with us.

As January 2005 began to slip away, in desperation, I broke down and sent Bethany a short letter at her non-profit organization's email address. It was my hope that enough time had passed where her heart might have softened a bit toward us. My letter stated how much we loved and missed her and that we were eager to welcome her back into our lives. It conveyed our willingness to work with her in creating a plan to repay her student loans so she could finish her degree. Even though the letter did not return to our mailbox, we had no way of knowing if she ever received or read it.

FIFTEEN

In March 2005 a letter came from the university addressed to Bethany. The envelope looked important so we opened it. It had been sent from an investigator for the Department of Equity and Diversity, and had been written in response to a complaint Bethany filed with their department. The letter described encounters their officers had with her on three occasions between September 2004 and January 2005.

Campus security guards had apparently responded to calls claiming someone had been seen in university buildings during winter break when those buildings were vacant and supposed to be locked. In one encounter, campus security found Bethany asleep in one of the buildings. The letter explained that she had not been stopped and questioned without cause. It stated she had introduced the topic of religion into the conversation. There was an account of how she had claimed to be affiliated with two different religions during two separate encounters. The letter went on to clearly state the university's harassment and discrimination policy. After an investigation, they concluded with a dismissal of Bethany's claim that officers had religiously harassed her. The letter also explained that they had not been able to get in touch with her as she had been "unwilling or unable" to provide a local address, contact information, or a valid student ID.

After receiving the disturbing letter, my husband called and spoke to a person from the University Department of Equity and Diversity. They were unable to give us any additional information about Bethany, and cited confidentially issues in that the letter had not been addressed to us.

On April 6, 2005, I copied a poem into my journal from a book of collected writings authored by people who waited for prodigal children to return.

"Perhaps She Will Land Upon That Shore"
>Perhaps she will land upon
>that shore,
>not in full sail
>but rather, a bit of broken
>wreckage for Him to gather.
>Perhaps He walks those shores
>Seeking such, who have
>believed a little, suffered
>much and so, been washed
>ashore.
>Perhaps of all the souls
>redeemed they most
>adore.

>Ruth Bell Graham
>London 1972

I read the poem over and over until I knew it by heart. I thought about the question I had answered while driving in January 2004: "Are you willing to wait as long as it takes for *her* good?"

We believed it was our task to wait, pray, trust, and somehow go on living. Often, we witnessed the closeness displayed in many of our friend's families. I especially noticed young women around Bethany's age as they faced the challenges in their developing careers, the excitement upon becoming engaged, and the joy of shopping for wedding gowns. During that time, as providence would have it, I was busy attending an unusually high number of wedding and baby showers. My husband and I also attended several weddings. All around us vibrant young people were happily living their lives.

Time was passing and we heard nothing more about Bethany's life. Our contacts were silent and although we regularly searched, there was nothing new on her organization's website. Though on one occasion, an Internet search led us to her picture in a group photo at a religious event. Her hair was quite long, and it was odd reconciling the updated image with the vision of her we carried in our minds. It was spring 2005 and I had last seen her three years earlier in May 2002 before she left for Africa. The last time her dad saw her was November 2003 right before she walked away in anger.

Both my husband and I tried to keep our minds busy, and continually looked for new projects to occupy our free time. I spent long hours in my flower garden during the summer of 2005. The beauty of nature brought a measure of comfort to my wounded heart.

There were many good people in our lives and we watched as several of them suffered through their own trials. We watched a young man go off to war in Iraq with pictures of his family tucked into the lining of his combat helmet, and once again we pondered the meaning of "family."

At any time of the day or night we were emotionally vulnerable to being thrown off guard by huge waves of grief and despair. There was no way to specifically predict what would set off these intense feelings, but I remember being strongly affected by catching a glimpse of a young mother holding a baby, or a fun-loving teenager laughing while shopping for shoes with her mother. Sometimes it was difficult just to be alive.

In early fall 2005, we received a phone call out of the blue from a person we did not know. He identified himself as one of Bethany's friends. He had not seen her for a long time and then unexpectedly ran into her on campus. Something about Bethany's demeanor and appearance bothered him enough that he was compelled to search the Internet to find her parents or at least a family member.

We were always grateful to hear from someone who could provide current information about her. He said she looked a bit disheveled, and during their conversation she responded to him in an evasive manner. He quietly listened while we described the details of our estrangement and communicated our own concerns. With great emphasis, we implored him not to tell Bethany he was in contact with us, as she would immediately cut him out of her life. He responded by making an offer to "unexpectedly" run into her a second time if it was at all possible. He said he would try to uncover specific information about her life and where she was living.

About a week later the young man encountered her again and we received a second phone call. He found that she spent a great deal of her time in one of the campus libraries. It was his impression that she seemed to be "stressed out" and struggling on a personal level. Unfortunately, Bethany did not reveal where she was living. We offered to send the young man money so he could take her out for a meal, and encouraged him to call us with any new information. He had a hard time understanding why we would not just "come and get her." But Bethany had made it extremely clear that she did not want us involved in any aspect of her life.

October 2005 marked Bethany's twenty-fourth birthday and three full years of estrangement. Being separated once again on our daughter's birthday brought a deeper dimension of sorrow to our hearts. But it was even worse knowing the passage of time had forced us into a new chapter of life lived totally without her. With each passing year we believed there was an increased likelihood of never seeing her face again.

Christmas 2005 arrived. Each holiday, birthday or milestone intensified the pain and stress we carried. Special days had become cruel markers in our tortured lives. We hungered to be with people we loved. That year we spent Christmas at home with our son and a few close family members and friends. I specifically remember that year because during our gift exchange, I pondered to myself "why" anyone would want to spend any time with us since our own daughter rejected us so completely. It continually felt as though we had something materially wrong with us as parents to have landed in such a position.

January 2006 marked a full seven years since Bethany first toured the university as a gifted high school senior. In our wildest imaginations, my husband and I could not have projected the series of events which had plunged us into such a merciless situation. I still clung to the hope that one day she would unexpectedly ring our doorbell. But harsh reality seemed to favor never seeing her again. Too much time had passed and too many things had happened. It seemed more likely that one day we would pick up the phone only to hear a police officer inform us that she was dead.

SIXTEEN

In April 2006, we were again in communication with the young man who found us on the Internet six months earlier. He had seen Bethany again and had introduced her to a few young women who studied at the university. As a result of this introduction, the young women befriended Bethany and extended invitations for her to spend time with them in their apartment.

In the young man's opinion, Bethany appeared paranoid and secretive, often changing her stories. Unfortunately, in one of his conversations with her, he made the mistake of mentioning that he had spoken to us. Bethany reacted by completely cutting him out of her life. However, he retained the relationships with the young women who had befriended Bethany. This gave him the ability to keep track of her in a limited, indirect way.

Every time we had a connection like this, we realized it held potential to help *or* harm Bethany. There was always great risk of her discovering that a trusted friend was actually "spying" on her and informing us about her life. We did not want our need for information to drive her into a state of "justified" paranoia and isolation. It was an impossible situation. But, if it had not been for people who randomly contacted us, we would have lost track of her entirely.

The young man believed Bethany was in need of a psychiatric evaluation. However, as we discussed this with him, we explained that she did not meet the guidelines which would force her into an emergency room evaluation. To our knowledge, and his, Bethany did not pose a danger to herself or others which was the qualifier for being involuntarily held and evaluated.

Through the young man, we had moved closer to Bethany's life than we had been in a long time. His concerns greatly escalated our fear and anxiety. Two and a half years had passed since she had sent us the threatening email and it had been six months since anyone had contacted us about her. As we looked into the future, we believed that we would eventually lose track of her and it frightened us. The last few people that knew her as a student would eventually get on with their lives and move away from the university area. Motivated by fear, we decided to directly reach out to her. Since Bethany had already cut the young man out of her life, we felt little would be lost by asking him to deliver a message to her from us.

Our message was an open invitation for Bethany to meet with me at the place of her choosing. It stipulated that I would only travel to see her if she wanted me to come. We hoped enough time had passed to decrease the intensity of her anger toward us and allow a short meeting. Our message was delivered but received no response. Once again we were left to deal with being rejected.

A few days later in April 2006, and right on the heels of our failed attempt to meet with Bethany, we received a very belated reply to an email we had sent to one of Bethany's friends three years earlier in 2003. We had tried to contact this woman just a few months after Bethany walked away from her dad on the university campus. In this belated reply, the woman said she was in the university area after living abroad. As one of Bethany's special friends, she expressed a desire to meet with her.

As we conversed with this individual over the Internet and telephone, we summarized everything we knew about Bethany's life and described our concerns. She was troubled to hear that Bethany was secluding herself from people who loved her. We knew our daughter deeply valued this woman's opinion and friendship. We hoped she would eagerly welcome her back into her life.

The woman said she would only be staying in the university area for a few days. However, she decided to contact as many of Bethany's former and current friends as she could so together they could hold an "intervention." It was her hope that if Bethany was directly confronted by a concerned group of old and new friends, she would admit to having a problem and agree to accept psychological counseling.

We provided this woman with the limited information we had about the people who contacted us on the Internet, and the "intervention" idea blossomed. It was a combined effort to join two totally different groups of people who were worried about Bethany. We were grateful for those who cared enough to go out of their way to reach out to our daughter. Due to Bethany's anger toward us, my husband and I knew we could not be directly involved in any sort of intervention.

We knew this type of encounter was extremely unpredictable and could backfire. Over and over again, Bethany had demonstrated a pattern of immediately distancing herself from conflict and never looking back. The act of gathering all her friends together in a room to confront her could trigger the unintended consequence of permanent separation from people who still loved and cared for her. Up to this point, nothing had broken her resolve to live life apart from her entire family and many people who genuinely loved her. We agreed with her friend that it was time to take a dramatic and bold approach in attempting to recover Bethany.

We offered to pay for a mental health professional to lead the intervention and any subsequent counseling Bethany might be willing to attend. It felt as though the tide was just on the brink of turning, as the love and compassion of many people was being powerfully harnessed to "rescue" her from herself. If Bethany could be made to realize she had a problem, we believed it would be the first step toward healing. Sadly, time ran out, and after much effort, the session never took place. We were crushed, and plunged into a helpless position. The estrangement would continue with no probable end in sight.

About one month later, in early May 2006, we received a series of emails from a person we did not know. She was connected to the female university students who had befriended Bethany. From this new contact we learned that a group of concerned students had come together and opened a bank account for Bethany which she could freely access as needed. They sensed that Bethany had unmet needs and responded by establishing this generous resource for her. The true source of the money was being concealed from Bethany, so she would not refuse to accept it. Reportedly, she was being told that the money was compensation for an academic "independent study" project which she was engaged in.

This new contact belonged to a group of compassionate people who seemed to truly care about our daughter. They were extending kindness. But, by concealing the true source of their financial assistance they were unwittingly feeding a delusion that Bethany was a type of paid university student or researcher. They asked us to partner with them by contributing enough funding to cover monthly rent checks which would anonymously pay Bethany's part of an apartment she would share with a few other women.

My husband and I were grateful for their compassion and conveyed our willingness to supply the monthly funding, but only under very clear terms. We stipulated that Bethany must be told the money was coming from us, and she must openly agree to receive it. Along with her consent to accept our money we added an additional stipulation requiring her to call us once a month to work toward the rebuilding of our relationship. We thought it was wrong to support her financially without her knowledge. This would be a flagrant violation of trust which would someday be revealed, giving her valid reason to never trust us again. Also, we believed that in anonymously paying her rent, we would become partners in creating a "pretend" world where she could live indefinitely in a sort of delusion. It was obvious she was struggling, but we did not want to put ourselves in a position of supporting her while at the same time perpetuating our estrangement.

The request for funding brought us to a breaking point, a distinct fork in the road, where we were pressed to make a very difficult choice. It was tempting, after such a long time, to provide for her in any sort of way.

After much agony and prayer, we made the decision not to send money to her without her knowledge, even though on the surface it looked like something we *should* do as parents. It was extremely painful to turn down this unusual, second-hand plea for help but we believed it to be the right choice. We hoped she would communicate with us, as we were more than willing to help her in a direct manner.

Due to the secrecy Bethany employed while dealing with friends, her legal right to confidentiality, and her rigid resolve to keep us out of her life, the true depth of her situation was not fully known. Since walking away from college she had effectively established a legitimate non-profit organization and had made several international trips. It was all very confusing. We did not completely understand why her life had fallen apart and had no way to predict if she would ever pull it back together again.

By deciding to withhold anonymous support, the connection we had with these compassionate people promptly disintegrated. It was May 2006 and Bethany was twenty-four years old. We prayed that God would protect her and lead her back to us, and that she would be granted the presence of mind to work out her issues in a realistic way.

SEVENTEEN

As May 2006 wore on, we noted the four-year anniversary date of Bethany's departure to Africa. After turning down the opportunity to reenter her life anonymously, we had a lot to process. Our hearts were heavy. It was tortuous to think about her unmet needs and her rigid resolve to keep us out of her life. We realized our decision could be interpreted by other people as not loving or caring about our daughter.

Together, my husband and I second-guessed our decision. But each time we talked it through, we landed at the same conclusion: we could not fund her anonymously. We also deliberated whether our desire to keep track of her through the years had just made things worse. If anything, she had been consistent in her rejection of us. Even though it was her legal right to live a life independent of family, it was difficult to think about her needs and dependence on others.

We found no new information about Bethany's non-profit organization on the Internet and our contacts had grown silent. The tide had turned and we were totally detached from our daughter.

The choice we had made set us on a new road to travel which would be a road of complete faith. We resolved to walk confidently into the future, trusting God to light our way.

I continued to copy verses and passages into my journal which soothed my heart and fed my spirit.

On August 2, 2006 I made the following entry:

"He will not crush the weakest reed or put out a flickering candle."
Isaiah 42:3

Although we could not know how life would turn out, we tried to embrace hope as we lived each day. People who knew us well seemed sympathetic to our plight and encouraged us to press on, but waves of deep grief continued to wash over us at unexpected times. Occasionally this would occur during my workday. Emotion would overtake me and I would pause, lay my head on my desk and just think. At work I was responsible for overseeing the health and welfare of so many disabled people, while at the same time I was powerless to help my own daughter. It was ironic and sad.

While living and working alongside others, my husband and I were affected by circumstances most people could never even think to imagine. Our position was bizarre and far beyond any "conventional" problems we heard about in most families. It seemed sensational, like the kind of story people watch in movies but never personally relate to. Overall, we opted not to discuss Bethany in public, but on the rare occasion when we did, we had to remind ourselves that people simply did not have the scope to really understand. Life felt better when we focused our attention on the lives of other people and the way their families were growing and changing.

On September 26, 2006, after almost four months of receiving no new information, we got an email from one of Bethany's closest friends. This was a person whom Bethany had greatly loved and respected. His message boldly stated his belief that God would not allow Bethany to fall beyond rescue, and how she would someday be restored. He expressed confidence that Bethany would remember fond memories of her childhood, the many people who loved her, and she would "break free and return." It was an unexpected message from a person who had not communicated with us for several years and it renewed our hope.

With the arrival of fall 2006, we were given the opportunity to host a graduate student who was in need of housing while completing a three-month internship in our town. The young woman was nearly the same age as Bethany. We were surprised at how easy it was to interact with her, and we quickly developed a close relationship, much like the relationship we had with our son. During those three months we enjoyed a wonderful gift of friendship. We were grateful to provide for someone in need, much in the same way other people had provided for Bethany. This lovely person brought sunshine into our lives and gave us an opportunity to "re-sharpen" our skills in relating to young adults.

Christmas 2006 marked the fifth winter holiday season without Bethany in our lives. We spent the holidays alone, just the two of us, as our son planned on visiting us in February. Through the passage of time, we had regained a small measure of peace in our daily lives. However, our thoughts often returned to our daughter and we longed to hear some word about how she was doing. We had communicated that we were willing to help. She knew how to reach us. So we continued to wait, and although we had hope, we could not imagine how her story was unfolding.

In early February 2007, right at the tail end of a major ice storm, our son came to visit us. Together, we spent four days enjoying the ice encrusted sights of our city, eating out and shopping. We were learning to be a family of three. We were beginning to laugh again and enjoy each other like a "normal" family would. But whenever we spent extended time with our son, the topic of Bethany always came up. We usually chose to limit conversation about her because there was never much to report and our son had his own version of suffering related to his own feelings about the situation. We believed our special time with him should focus on his young life, as we wanted him to understand how much we cared about his plans and dreams for the future.

At the conclusion of our son's visit, we drove him back to the airport. All the ice from the storm was gone and we looked forward to the promise of spring. Everything was on the brink of change, and when we stepped outside we could smell it and feel it.

On the morning of March 3, 2007 we attended a memorial service for a dear friend. It was a Saturday. The service concluded in the early afternoon and we drove home to spend the rest of the day relaxing and doing things around the house. As we entered our kitchen we noticed the message light on our answering machine was blinking, indicating a new message. Messages were a common occurrence in our home and my husband casually pushed the button to listen. Both of us fell instantly into a stunned silence as we heard a man identify himself as a police officer and inquire if we were the parents of Bethany Yeiser. The message stated that she was in police custody near her university. The officer stated a phone number and directed us to call back at our earliest convenience.

The message struck us like a lightning bolt and shook us to the core. However we were quick to realize that by being taken into in police custody, Bethany was not dead.

We did not know how many hours had passed since the message had been left and we were aware of a three-hour time zone difference. We were in shock and desperate to know what was happening. I dialed the number and listened to the phone ring over and over again. I kept waiting and no one answered. I hung up, redialed, and still no one answered. Then we tried a different approach by using operator assistance to connect us to the general number for the city police. Finally, a person answered and said they were having problems with their entire phone system.

It took a series of transfers to many different people at many different phone extensions to finally reach an officer who had specific information about Bethany. He explained that two of his officers had responded to a call in the morning from a woman who lived near a churchyard. She had heard screaming, and had seen a young woman hitting herself, so she called the police. The person screaming had been Bethany.

The responding officers reportedly questioned Bethany. After assessing her mental status, they determined she posed a danger to herself. This qualified her for a trip to the emergency room for expert psychiatric evaluation. She was transported by squad car and was being legally detained at the hospital. The officer gave me a phone number for a police social worker and encouraged me to call right away. My husband hurriedly placed a blank piece of paper and a pen in front of me so I could record the names and phone numbers of the people I was talking with. We were both struggling to keep our minds clear.

I am so thankful for the police social worker I spoke to on that day. He was kind and patient, allowing me enough time to give a short history of Bethany's life, a summary of how she had fallen on hard times, and how for many years had completely cut friends and family out of her life. I told him we were relieved to know she was safe and in a place where she would be psychiatrically evaluated. The social worker carefully explained the psychiatric hold process. Bethany could be held for up to 72 hours against her will. However, he said if she was able to convince the emergency room psychiatrist that she was mentally stable, she could be released much sooner. The 72-hour hold had begun at 10 AM Saturday morning. The social worker clarified that an "emergency conservatorship" or guardianship would be granted through the legal system if Bethany was determined to be mentally unstable. In that case she could be legally held for 14 to 30 days. I tried to keep track of everything he was saying, but the information and terms were becoming jumbled together in my mind. The situation was overwhelmingly stressful and horrifying.

The police social worker gave me clear and exact instructions on how to proceed. He explained that due to privacy rules, I could not request information about Bethany from hospital staff without her permission, and I would probably be told she was not even listed as a patient in the emergency room. He said I should tell the receptionist I had been notified directly by the police and knew my daughter was being held for psychiatric assessment. Additionally, I was to state that despite privacy laws, I retained the legal right to report information to them about Bethany's life.

We felt great urgency to communicate with the emergency room physician as soon as possible. We did not want Bethany to be released without a psychiatrist being made fully aware of her history and the way her life had severely deteriorated.

I called the hospital and was connected to the emergency room receptionist. I communicated exactly what the police social worker told me to say. The receptionist seemed pleased to be in touch with one of Bethany's family members and directly transferred me to the physician on duty. I was amazed at how quickly I had been connected to the doctor.

There was limited time to talk, so I gave a quick summary of Bethany's life, her decline, and how she had completely cut almost everyone she knew out of her life over a span of four and a half years. I mentioned Bethany's published scientific articles to the doctor along with the fact that she had dropped out of college, traveled all over the world, and had become secretive about her life with her very few remaining friends. I explained that to our knowledge she had never used alcohol or drugs, and she had been fundamentally against putting any sort of unnecessary chemicals into her body. She had even been reluctant to take aspirin unless it was absolutely necessary. With great urgency I pled with the doctor not to release her. She had fallen into a safety net and we could not bear the thought of her being released without some sort of intervention to prevent further decline.

After speaking with me less than ten minutes, the doctor agreed to admit Bethany to an off-site psychiatric unit and explained that she would be transferred to that unit by ambulance later in the day. Hospital admission would assure a comprehensive psychiatric evaluation and a treatment plan. I was reminded that she could only be kept against her will for up to 72 hours. Then the doctor paused and said she appeared to be homeless, and judging by her appearance, she looked to have been "out there" for quite some time. He said Bethany had been talkative and was cooperating with hospital staff. He also said he would ask her if she was willing to speak to us, and if so, we could call her on an emergency room phone. I was then put on hold to be connected with a hospital social worker.

While on hold I brought my husband up to speed on everything I had learned and we discussed the possibility of flying out to see Bethany the following day. We understood the serious and urgent nature of the unfolding events, but at the same time, nothing seemed real. Bethany had become ill, homeless, and was awaiting transfer to a psychiatric hospital. The magnitude of it all was crushing, and way too much to fully comprehend. Time pressed against us as the clock marked the hours and minutes remaining on the 72-hour hold.

A few minutes after speaking with the emergency room physician, I was connected to a hospital social worker. She informed me Bethany had agreed to speak with us on the phone and had signed a release which allowed the hospital to share her medical information with us. I was given contact information for the psychiatric facility where Bethany would be transferred along with the number to an emergency room phone where I could reach Bethany. The social worker was uncertain how long it would be until her transfer to the off-site unit across town.

I hung up and stared at the paper in front of me. In less than one hour we had arrived home, received the message from the police, spoke to a police officer, a police social worker, an emergency room physician, and a hospital social worker. On the paper I had written words that included "72-hour hold," "hospital will make application for emergency conservatorship," "hospital stay can extend 14-30 days," "need to get her medical benefits," and the words "classic schizophrenia."

Life had exploded into a frenzy of jagged pieces, temporarily suspended in the atmosphere around us. The moment I hung up the phone, we began to feel the impact as they all crashed down upon us. We had no way of knowing the degree of permanent damage the jagged pieces would inflict, as a sequence of troubled thoughts raced through our minds. Just how sick was Bethany? How could they know for sure she was "homeless," and "could she REALLY have schizophrenia?" We wondered if we even knew her anymore. The description of this person sounded nothing like the Bethany we had once known. It had been too many years since we had experienced any sort of normal relationship with her. We were devastated and did not know what to think.

There was no question that we needed to see her right away if she was in agreement. It would take time to become reacquainted and rebuild trust with each other. Because of this we planned to stay at least five days.

We went into our bedroom so I could collect myself and get into a comfortable position before dialing the phone to speak with Bethany. I was nervous, cold, and my hands were trembling. We reviewed our plans, and then I dialed the number. The phone rang a few times and then suddenly I heard her voice on the other end saying "hello." I simply said, "Hi Bethany, this is Mom." She sounded delighted to hear my voice and began conversing like we had just spoken the day before. She explained that she was in an emergency room affiliated with her university, and that university police had been very nice to her in the morning, driving her to the hospital just to get "checked out."

Bethany spoke very rapidly as she clarified that the hospital emergency room was not located on the main campus, but across town and affiliated with the university school of medicine. Pointing out the affiliation to the university seemed especially important to her. She sounded happy and excited and asked how we were doing. I briefly updated her about our lives. I told her it was good to hear her voice and asked if she would like us to come and see her. Without hesitation she agreed to a visit. When I said we would try to see her the next day, she seemed very surprised it would be so soon. She voiced concern about where we would meet her as she expected to be discharged that same day. I chose to ignore her comment and acted like I had no idea she was being held against her will. I asked her to hold on a moment while I quickly shared with my husband her consent to meet us. He immediately left for his office to make the travel arrangements.

Bethany and I continued to converse, and while she spoke I could sense things were not right with her. She seemed too "upbeat" after living through the events of the day. After all, only a few hours had passed since she had been screaming for some reason and had been transported in a police car. This type of scenario would crush most people, but she seemed quite energized. The whole situation was strange.

My head was spinning, and I treaded lightly throughout the conversation because I did not know what to expect next. After only a few minutes of speaking with her, she was interrupted by someone in the emergency room. She told me she was needed for a blood test and would have to hang up the phone. Then she asked if I would call her back in about ten minutes because she was enjoying our conversation and had nothing else to do while she waited for test results.

I agreed to call her back and hung up. I put the phone down, fell back into the bed, and stared at the circles of textured pattern stamped into the plaster of our bedroom ceiling. I was physically and emotionally drained. While continuing to stare at the ceiling, I allowed my mind to fall into a "neutral" mode. The raised patterns appeared to invert after a while due to a change of perspective. The longer I stared at the pattern the more distinctly it appeared to be inverted. It was almost like focusing on one of those hidden pictures that look like a senseless mess of colorful spots in a frame. When you stare long enough and relax your eyes, the picture finally appears. As I continued to lie there, I knew the ceiling was merely a focal point allowing my mind to catch up from an onslaught of extreme stress.

During those ten minutes while I waited to call again, I imagined the countless ways our lives could and would change. The sudden and unexpected reappearance of Bethany with a serious mental illness threatened every aspect of our lives. The whole situation was chilling. I wondered if I would have to quit my job to watch over her, or if both of us would have to quit our jobs and maybe even move to another state. I had no idea what to expect and the insecurity of it all frightened me.

When ten minutes had passed I redialed the phone. Again Bethany answered and we continued to talk. She kept saying how good it was to be speaking with me again and I shared with her that her father and I deeply missed her. She mentioned how much she enjoyed living in her city and occasionally made a fleeting reference to her "home." I avoided digging too deep with my questions because I did not want her to feel threatened. We mainly discussed common topics she introduced from the past. After conversing quite a long time I told her I would have to hang up because it was getting late and I still had to pack my suitcase for the trip we hoped to take in the morning.

After hanging up I called the number for the off-site psychiatric facility where Bethany would be transferred and asked to speak with a physician. As soon as he answered, I explained that my daughter was a patient scheduled for transport to the facility in a matter of hours and I wished to give a comprehensive report on her history. I felt it was important for the physician to know about her past, and everything I had just learned about her current situation.

My main goal in sharing information was to decrease the chance of an early discharge. I wanted to be sure Bethany would receive a comprehensive evaluation and any treatment she needed. I was concerned because since Bethany was so well spoken, I feared she might convince them that she had been admitted in error. The physician on duty patiently listened, conveyed thanks for the information and scheduled a time where we could meet and talk with the supervising psychiatrist on the following day.

During an earlier phone conversation, the hospital social worker had requested we bring a few changes of clothing for Bethany to wear during her stay on the psychiatric unit. I had learned that she had arrived at the emergency room in a very dirty outfit. Even though Bethany had not lived with us for years, I had to spontaneously produce an assortment of things for her to wear.

My husband had not yet returned from his office with the flight arrangements and I had no idea how soon we would have to depart for the airport, so I pulled out a big suitcase and rapidly began to pack.

My mind was racing as I tried to concentrate enough to think of everything I might need during the five days we expected to be gone. Then I dragged boxes out of closets which contained items Bethany left behind when she moved out of our home in August 1999. Between the few articles of clothing I found in boxes, and by adding a few things of my own, I was able to put together a small wardrobe which I hoped would fit her. I also included several personal items I anticipated she would need in a hospital setting. It was a frantically systematic packing job.

While I filled my suitcase, my mind struggled to reconcile the cruel details of a new dimension of reality. After watching Bethany work so hard throughout the years to achieve high academic standing, and after all we had contributed toward her hopes and dreams, somehow she had landed in a psychiatric hospital, seriously ill and presumed homeless.

My husband arrived home and looked like a beaten man. He placed the plane reservations on the kitchen counter and informed me that our flight was scheduled for 6 AM the following morning, which was less than 12 hours away. We were both in shock and could barely stop to comfort each other. The clock was ticking and we had to finish packing, attempt to sleep, and get up before three AM to catch our morning flight. Infused with adrenaline, we were overwhelmed on every level.

EIGHTEEN

Our alarm clock went off at 2:30 AM and we shot out of bed like robots. There were many loose ends to tie up at the last minute before our unexpected five-day trip, and although we had barely slept, a fresh surge of adrenaline pushed us forcefully into the new day. We had booked a Sunday morning flight out of Dayton, which was about an hour from our home. We decided to depart early in case we encountered delays with traffic and airport security.

It was four in the morning and it felt like the dead of night as we pulled out of our driveway. It had recently rained and the moon reflected brightly off the wet pavement. As we crossed over the expressway toward the entry ramp, we noticed an unusual amount of very slow-moving westbound traffic. As soon as our car entered the eastbound expressway ramp, we understood the reason for the backed up traffic. Black ice covered the road. My husband immediately slowed down to avoid skidding. Although eastbound traffic was very light, abandoned cars peppered the roadside. We were quick to realize that our primary goal was changed from getting to the airport to just staying on the road.

While slowly passing an alarming number of stranded cars, we began to see emergency vehicles and tow trucks in the distance. Despite dangerous conditions, we decided to ignore our first opportunity to exit the expressway. Together, we were determined to keep moving forward until we could go no further.

Slowly and carefully, and with anxious thoughts, we crept along, calculating miles traveled against miles yet to go. It was obvious that by driving at such a slow speed, we would never get to the airport on time. And it was extraordinary, at such a critical time, that weather would be the singular factor to prevent our long-awaited reunion with Bethany.

Disappointed, we kept moving forward, wondering when we too, would slip off the road and join the stranded cars. Time and miles continued to crawl by. Then after a while, we began to notice the cars ahead of us were slowly increasing their speed. Miles were ticking by at a quicker pace, and we recalculated time and distance. Although realizing our situation was still quite impossible, we kept moving forward.

After several more miles the road suddenly opened up and we began to move at a normal speed. Once again we recalculated and discovered we had a marginal chance of catching our flight. We arrived with just enough time to park the car, clear security, run to the gate, and board the plane. Amazingly, despite chaos all around us, we were protected and provided for.

While settling into our seats on the plane, we began to let down a bit. The icy drive had put us on edge, intensifying a monumental level of stress. We faced a long flight and needed to rest, but we also needed to talk. We had an enormous amount of information to process from the day before and so much to face as soon as we landed. We discussed and listed things we hoped to accomplish, and began compiling a written timeline of Bethany's early life and her descent into what we now understood to be true mental illness.

Despite all we had endured through the years, and all we had just learned, there was a place in my mind where I held a secret hope. I wondered if it was possible, against all reason, that Bethany was really okay and all she needed to do was simply choose a return to normal life. And yet, I fully realized that by being admitted into a psychiatric unit she would likely be labeled with a significant psychiatric diagnosis.

The limited amount of rest and relaxation we experienced during the flight was quickly replaced by another surge of adrenaline as we stepped out of the plane. We had arrived, and due to the time zone difference it was still morning. We collected our luggage and boarded a bus which transported us to a car rental agency.

When we arrived at the rental agency, I sat outside on a cement bench with our luggage while my husband went inside to sign paperwork and collect car keys. As I sat there, it felt as though I had been transported into an entirely different world. The air was hot and dry and a strong wind blew against a row of palm trees in front of a car dealership across the street. People walking by were immersed in their daily lives. A few appeared excited to be on vacation and others casually strolled onward to their next destination. I remembered times in our lives when we were just like them, simply going about the business of living.

We climbed into our rental car and opened a map. We were hot, tired, and unfamiliar with the part of the city where the psychiatric hospital was located. Tenuously we pulled out of the parking lot and found our way to the expressway. As we merged into extremely heavy traffic, we wondered how late we would be for our scheduled meeting with the psychiatrist.

After weaving in and out of heavy traffic for over an hour and missing an exit, we somehow arrived in time for the meeting. We were both very quiet as we got out of the car and began to walk across the parking lot encircling the small hospital. Life had become unreal, and it felt like we were actors in a poignant scene of a play, just acting a part. I remember speaking out loud, just like a narrator would: "So here we are walking across the parking lot of a psychiatric hospital, preparing to see our daughter."

As we approached the building, a woman walked toward us who appeared to be an employee just finishing her shift. When she drew closer, she smiled and said, "You are obviously the parents of our new blonde patient." Taken off guard by her statement, we responded by saying "Yes, that seems to be the case," even though Bethany's hair had always been more of a light auburn color.

We entered the facility and proceeded through a security process before being allowed to enter the locked unit. A guard searched all our belongings. He paid special attention to the clothing and personal items I had brought for Bethany. In order to comply with hospital rules which restricted anything that could be used as a weapon or a tool for committing suicide, such as a belt, I had to cut the drawstrings off one pair of pants. As soon as all items were cleared, we sat in the waiting room while the psychiatrist was notified of our arrival.

My husband and I were silent, deep in our own thoughts. After a relatively short but uncomfortable period of time, we were ushered down a series of long corridors and locked doors. At the end of a hall we entered a conference room with a large table. The head psychiatrist introduced himself to us along with a young psychiatry resident. He said the resident would assist in Bethany's treatment. Both of them were friendly and professional. They attempted to help us feel comfortable in a very awkward situation. Then we sat around the table and started to talk.

Together, my husband and I summarized Bethany's early life including the events that had transpired since taking her to college to begin her freshman year. Both doctors listened attentively and asked a lot of questions. We noticed that they were not only interested in Bethany's history, but also in us, and in the dynamic of our family relationships. When we completed our story, the psychiatrist looked directly at both of us and said, "What happened to Bethany was not your fault." The statement caught us off guard as it was the last thing we expected to hear from anyone, especially a psychiatrist.

We had carried a burden of guilt because we had not understood that Bethany was mentally ill. Silently, illness had slowly gripped her mind, and in our ignorance our perspective had become warped. Everything had become horribly tangled and beyond sorting out.

The psychiatrist informed us that after considering initial medical and psychiatric assessments, Bethany's diagnosis was determined to be schizophrenia with psychosis. He provided a detailed explanation of the symptoms and a typical biological progression of the illness. Then he paused and encouraged us to refocus our thoughts about her future. Any scholastic expectations we still held for her needed to be "lowered" as her prognosis did not favor a complete recovery. It was impossible to fully comprehend the grievous information and the impact it would have on all of our lives.

Blood work had been completed and a CT scan was scheduled for the next day. Additionally, a low dose of Risperdal, a medication commonly used to treat schizophrenia had been prescribed. The psychiatrist was hopeful Bethany would respond well to the drug as she had no history of alcohol, marijuana, or street drugs which can chemically damage the brain and complicate treatment. While we accepted the diagnosis of schizophrenia, we were informed that Bethany *had not* accepted it, and therefore she was refusing to take the medication.

Antipsychotic medication was expected to ease Bethany's symptoms and help her gain insight into her illness. Our biggest fear was that she would be discharged from the hospital without understanding that she was mentally ill. If this happened, her condition would continue to decline in a profound way.

The psychiatrists informed us that they planned on petitioning the court in order to extend her hospitalization beyond the initial 72-hour hold. They projected she would remain in the psychiatric unit for several weeks. This gave us a great sense of relief. She was in a safe place, surrounded by caring people with the skill and resources to essentially save her life.

In regard to Bethany's presumed homelessness, the psychiatrist said her physical appearance suggested she had been on the streets for quite some time. By hearing this statement from two separate physicians in just a matter of hours, our emotional capacity began to shut down. Instinctive self-preservation took over. We were left functioning mainly on an academic level. The enormity of the situation was more than we could bear.

As the meeting began to wind down, the psychiatrist suggested that when Bethany was eventually discharged, we should plan on taking her back to Ohio to live with us. The enormity of the suggestion caught us off guard and we became defensive. It was an option we had not fully processed and could not instantly embrace. Bethany was an adult and had not lived in our home for many years. Until just the day before, she had done everything in her power to keep us out of her life, even falsely accusing us of mistreating her. We could not imagine that she would ever consent to moving in with us. Secondly, when she had been well, she was most fulfilled by being part of an academic community. If we moved her into our suburban neighborhood she would be "safe," but would certainly smother from boredom and the feeling of being "trapped" by once again living with parents.

It was mid-afternoon and our session with the psychiatrists drew to a close. We informed the physicians we were in the process of compiling a written timeline of Bethany's life. We hoped the document would broaden their understanding of her individuality and intelligence. As the meeting ended we were given the opportunity to reunite with our daughter. We left the conference room severely shaken by the harsh and serious nature of Bethany's situation and ours.

An incredibly long chapter of painful estrangement was nearly at an end. It was unfolding in a way we could never have imagined. We were both tremendously anxious as we prepared to see her. Both psychiatrists walked with us down a series of corridors and into a locked wing of the hospital. The walk ended right outside the door to the community room.

NINETEEN

The door of the community room was ajar. Hesitantly we stepped inside. The overcrowded space was alive with loud, active patients. Right in the center of all the activity stood a very thin, delicate looking young woman with straight, chin length hair, and blue eyes. She was dressed in faded aqua colored hospital attire and white socks. When I looked into her face my brain was forced to make a major adjustment as the image carried in my mind for so many years was quite different from the person who stood before me. The psychiatrists stood back in the doorway and watched as my husband and I slowly approached Bethany. Spontaneously, the three of us met in a long emotional embrace. This small person was indeed our daughter, and after waiting so many long and painful years, it was wonderful to hold her in our arms.

Bethany became nervous and jumped right into conversation as though little time had passed since we had all been together. She kept repeating how good it was to see us, and that she loved us. We expressed our love for her along with our relief in finally seeing her again. None of us mentioned the events which had broken our relationship.

When I stated it had been five long years since I last saw her, she looked at me with surprise and said it could not possibly have been that long. I briefly reminded her of our last parting in May 2002, right before she traveled to Africa and the current date of March 2007. She paused to look at me while appearing to consider my statement, and then seemed to reluctantly accept it. As we continued to talk she spoke rapidly and seemed pressured to keep the conversation moving along. She also mentioned her grief from what she had witnessed in Africa. I had a hard time gauging her emotions, as at times she was smiling and then suddenly I wondered if she was going to cry.

I asked about her hair because I had never seen it so light. She said she spent a lot of time outdoors, and sun exposure had naturally lightened it. Her face appeared sunburned and she had a few red marks on her nose. She seemed embarrassed and nervous about being hospitalized and said she was healthy and only being checked out as a result of a misunderstanding. Despite the baggy hospital gown and pants, I could not help but notice how thin she had become. Her arms, wrists and hands looked so small and weak it was hard to believe this same person had played the violin with strength and passion.

Bethany seemed surprised to learn we planned on staying in the area until Friday. She said she was concerned about how we would find each other after her discharge, because she wanted to see us again before we returned home. She told us she enjoyed living in the city and was eager to return to her "home," which she clarified was no longer located on the university campus. We asked about her non-profit organization and she gave us an elusive answer. When she began to describe how she spent much of her time tending a church garden, we sensed some defensiveness on her part and decided to switch topics.

She was pleasant and friendly, but seemed a bit on edge, so we exercised caution in probing any deeper into her life. During this first meeting we continued to assure her of our love and did not allude to the emotional pain we endured for so many years.

Because the psychiatrist had advised us to keep our first visit short, our time with her came quickly to an end. Upon arriving at the unit we had surrendered the bag of clothing we had brought for her so it could be inventoried. When I informed her that we brought things for her to wear, she seemed a little surprised and reminded us of her imminent discharge. She politely thanked us and we reluctantly parted with the promise of returning the next day, Monday, for both the afternoon and evening visiting sessions.

On our way out of the building one of the older security guards complimented us about our nice daughter and described an enjoyable Ping-Pong game he had played with her the night before. He then suggested we bring her some sandals, as he said it would help her be more comfortable during her hospitalization.

After beginning our day at three in the morning and driving through ice, flying across the country, meeting with psychiatrists and finally reuniting with our daughter, our physical endurance was severely depleted and our emotions were ragged. So many times over the years we had imagined what a reunion with Bethany would be like but we never could have envisioned the scenario we had just lived through.

We left the hospital and found a restaurant for a quick dinner, and then proceeded to search for a grocery store. We recognized the enormous amount of stress we were under and decided to purchase a supply of food we could carry with us and eat in a hurry. Somehow we had to survive at least physically through the remainder of the week. In the grocery store we wandered down unfamiliar isles and somehow found what we needed. With our task completed, all that was left for us to do was to drive to the hotel and check into our room.

Once we settled in we called our son and my sister. It was terrible reconstructing the call we received on Saturday from the police, our treacherous drive through the ice, and the long flight which delivered us to Bethany, held against her will in a psychiatric hospital.

On Monday morning we awoke to the horror of reality and began to plan our day. My husband tried to go online at the hotel and found he could not remember his email password. It was the same password he used multiple times every single day for months, but he simply could not bring it to mind. The overload of stress erased it from his memory. Without ready access to email he was disconnected from his work responsibilities and had no idea if there were outstanding issues requiring immediate attention.

Due to time zone differences we both decided to leave voicemail messages at our jobs. The message I left for my supervisor simply stated a family emergency. I would not report to work all week, but would follow up with a phone call to explain later. With a new day stretching before us, we decided our main goal for the morning was to somehow collect Bethany's mail. At our initial meeting she disclosed that she had not picked up mail for many months. She had given us permission to collect it for her, if it was even possible.

Traffic was legendarily heavy in the city and it took about an hour each way to drive between the hospital and the university area. Bethany's mailbox was located in a privately owned business right on the edge of the campus. It was the exact same place, located near stores and restaurants, where three and a half years earlier her dad sat all day hoping to find her.

Our time was limited as we had early afternoon commitments at the hospital, but we felt an urgency to collect her mail and find out all we could about her legal and financial matters. We especially wanted to know if she had any outstanding legal issues with the federal government in regard to donations made to her non-profit organization. When we arrived at the establishment, we presented the attendant with our identification cards and introduced ourselves. We explained we had flown in from out of town because our daughter was very ill and in the hospital. Then we asked the attendant if he remembered Bethany.

He was quick to respond that he certainly did remember her. We watched as this older gentleman attempted to hold back his emotions, while expressing deep concern about her being ill. He said he had been worried because she suddenly stopped collecting her mail. He described how he kind of "looked out" for her as he had sensed she was struggling. Even though she had not paid her mailbox rent for many months, he faithfully continued to collect and store her mail, hoping she would eventually return. With tears in his eyes he said he was relieved knowing we were in town to help her. We paid the overdue fees, were given a very large bundle of mail, and thanked him for caring so much about our daughter.

My husband carried the mail to a cement bench near the middle of a busy courtyard. We found ourselves sitting on the exact same bench my husband occupied throughout the long day in November 2003 when he went looking for her.

Due to the gravity of Bethany's situation we started opening the envelopes. We found an abundance of student loan default notices from different accounts in varying amounts, totaling far more than we had anticipated. Bank statements listed overdue fees on a safe deposit box. There was some mail for her non-profit but we found no evidence of outstanding legal issues. Near the bottom of the stack I found a few personal letters and a Christmas card we had mailed more than a year before. I knew one envelope held a fifty dollar bill and a note conveying love and prayers for her safe return. I cried when I realized she never received the messages I had so carefully written with prayerful hope.

As we sorted through the overwhelming number of overdue notices and statements, we fell deeper and deeper into the enormity of her situation. Near the bottom of the pile we came upon a letter from the police department. In it we found an outdated summons for trespassing on university property. Bethany had failed to appear in court which had generated a warrant for her arrest.

Stricken by grief and shock, we stood up to leave. As hundreds of students streamed past us, we paused, held each other and wept. Bombarded with so much dreadful information, life felt unreal. Silently we walked back to our car then slowly wove into the heavy traffic to make the hour-long drive across town to the psychiatric hospital. We were due for a second meeting with the psychiatrists before meeting Bethany for the early afternoon visiting hour.

We cleared security and were once again ushered into a conference room. The psychiatrists reported that Bethany was continuing to refuse medication and most of her time was spent alone in her room. She also refused to participate in group therapy sessions. We asked if the facility had a piano and discovered that there was one located in the basement. We encouraged the psychiatrist to provide Bethany with an opportunity to play, as this would give her something to do. We also had interest in knowing if she had been able to retain her musical skill in spite of her illness.

We continued to discuss Bethany's situation with the psychiatrists. After much thought and consideration, my husband and I had come to realize, the safest and most practical option was for her to move into our home. If she would agree, we could help assure her ongoing treatment and encourage her recovery. Despite the risks we believed this to be the best plan but knew it hinged entirely on her legal right to choose. She was twenty-five years old and had lived an independent life for nearly eight years, so we expected she would not willingly agree to this option.

Due to the seriousness nature of her situation, we knew it would be a huge adjustment for all of us if she consented to move into our home. Things were changing so quickly, it felt as though we were being swept off our feet. Thankfully, we were allowed to relax a bit when the doctor projected that Bethany would most likely remain hospitalized a few more weeks in order for her to become stabilized on medication. We needed time to process everything that was happening.

When our meeting with the psychiatrists concluded early on Monday afternoon, we were again escorted down the series of locked corridors which led to the same community room where we reunited with Bethany the day before. She was waiting for us and wore a pair of jeans and a casual top. The clothes hung loosely on her small frame. We hugged her and gave her a small bag containing two oranges. Because it was our second meeting we felt a bit more relaxed. We pushed a few chairs into a corner of the room so we could talk. Since the room was relatively small and crowded with many intrusive patients, we found it challenging to speak with any semblance of privacy. Bethany thanked us for the oranges and began eating them. She said the hospital food was good and she especially enjoyed the breakfasts and desserts.

Sitting across from us was an older middle-aged couple with a young man who appeared to be their son. He was slumped into a chair directly facing the couple and had his legs propped up on the woman's lap. He appeared extremely sleepy and struggled to keep his eyes open. The woman stroked and comforted the young man as he attempted to communicate in a type of drugged state. The man and woman appeared to speak soft words of encouragement to the patient although they both looked to be quite concerned and upset themselves.

A television set in a corner of the room played a loud cartoon type of program until two patients began to take turns changing the channel in heated disagreement. The room was alive with disorganized activity. A few patients kept coming up to us trying to divert our attention to them, so we had to be a bit rude in deflecting their requests in order to carry on a coherent conversation with our daughter.

We updated Bethany about her brother's life, our home and our current jobs. When we mentioned her grandfather's death in 2004, it did not seem to surprise her. We went on to discuss other extended family members she had not seen in many years and she appeared interested in hearing what everyone was doing.

We were cautious in introducing topics which might cause conflict, but ventured a few questions about where she actually lived. She was guarded and elusive about providing specific information, and we began to feel as though we had breached an unseen barrier. She wistfully mentioned her home where she longed to return, and recalled times when she had taken the opportunity to do some camping which she described as similar to our family vacations. It was not clear to us whether she had done this camping with a group of people or alone. Several times during our conversation she mentioned how much she enjoyed living in the university area.

We could sense she was starting to feel uncomfortable with our questions so we changed the topic to fun times spent as a family in the home where she and her brother grew up. We reminded her about the pool in our backyard and the swimming she used to enjoy with friends. As we talked more specifically about memories and people, a surprised but quizzical expression seemed to brighten her face as she slowly said, "Yes, I remember them." As we continued to reminisce, she seemed to recall more and more details. It appeared as if she was actively stepping out of clouded thinking and into the clear presence of reality. It was a fascinating thing to witness. It was like her brain was unlocking areas which had been suppressed and forgotten for a very long time. Our conversation seemed to revive treasured memories which caused the remaining time to pass very quickly. As all visitors were being ushered out of the room, we hugged her and promised to return later in the day for the evening visiting hour.

While walking out of the hospital at the end of our afternoon visit on Monday, our thoughts immediately returned to the outstanding arrest warrant we discovered in Bethany's mail. We hurried into our car and headed toward the university with an urgent desire to meet with campus security. Upon our arrival at the campus, a university employee directed us to a building near the outer perimeter of the college grounds.

We parked our rental car across the street from the security building and proceeded through a crosswalk packed with students on their way to and from classes. We entered the building and requested a meeting with the head security officer. During our wait, we visited with the receptionist who also happened to be an officer. When we briefly described our daughter's situation to the receptionist, he casually classified Bethany's "type" as commonplace. He expounded upon the fact that a large number of young people, having once been enrolled at the university, ended up defaulting into the category of "nuisance" people. This was an awful concept to consider, and we envisioned a multitude of ruined lives which seemed to be an everyday occurrence as far as security was concerned.

Eventually we were ushered into a private office where a young, friendly man greeted us as we introduced ourselves. When we mentioned Bethany's name, the officer seemed surprised and said that he knew her. He easily recalled several instances where she had been confronted after being found in restricted areas of the campus. He said it had been a while since he last saw her and then described her frequent pattern of walking down the public sidewalk directly across from the security office and right on the edge of the campus.

He said our daughter was known to alter her appearance in the way she dressed, and mentioned a period of time when she had become easily recognizable by wearing a long green dress and a head covering. He said most of the officers knew her and were aware of a court order restricting her from being on university property. He seemed relieved to hear about her hospitalization and our intention to move her back to Ohio. In regard to Bethany's outstanding warrant, he suggested we find a lawyer who specialized in student issues. As we traded business cards, the officer extended his willingness to assist us in any way possible within the realm of his job.

We left the security office and headed across campus toward the main library in order to access a computer. We felt an urgency to find contact information on lawyers who might be willing to advise us.

It was painful to walk into the campus library while Bethany was being held across town in a psychiatric unit. We believed it was one of her favorite places and it felt surreal and horribly wrong to be there without her. On the main floor, I took a moment to gaze across an expansive area packed with hundreds of students studying intently at small desks. In my mind I envisioned Bethany as a student, right there in the room, researching and typing her school papers. Then I remembered that after dropping out of school, she had reportedly worked through the night on many occasions in order to obtain tax-exempt status for her non-profit organization. The campus library was her world where her life had begun to blossom, but illness had silently consumed her, dragging her into a devastating descent until she seemed to forget everything and everyone she once held dear.

We logged into a library computer and searched for local attorneys specializing in student issues. My husband and I discussed our specific questions and then I dialed one of the numbers. After giving a brief explanation of Bethany's situation to the law firm receptionist, I was connected to a lawyer. He agreed to allow me just a minute of his time in order to determine if he was interested in assisting us, and if we were willing to pay a five thousand dollar retainer fee. The lawyer then proceeded to imply that our daughter was just another one of the "rich kids" attending the university, and I was just another one of those parents willing to throw money at lawyers to make legal matters disappear. I promptly ended the conversation and conveyed the information to my husband. Right then and there we made the decision to choose a public defender.

Late in the afternoon on that Monday, we drove away from the university in the direction of the hospital. Even though we were engulfed by congested rush hour traffic, we decided there was still enough time to find a store where we could purchase a pair of sandals for Bethany and also grab a quick dinner before the early evening visiting hour.

After a short search we found an enclosed shopping mall, parked the car and entered one of the stores. We were tired, hot, and emotionally weary. As we stepped into the bright and cool mall environment, it felt as though we had entered a foreign land. We had become so immersed in the world of psychiatry, mental illness, and the heartbreak of Bethany's shattered life, we had forgotten all about normal living. As we looked for sandals in several different stores I found it almost impossible to make a decision on which pair we should buy. The immense amount of stress we were experiencing confounded my ability to make a quick decision on the purchase of even a simple pair of sandals.

On Monday evening we arrived at the hospital carrying a pair of black sandals and a slice of French silk pie.

Although it was only our third trip to the hospital, we found it remarkable how quickly we had adapted to the security process which had seemed so invasive just the day before. The hospital protocol and several of the staff members had become unexpectedly familiar to us.

Before joining a security guard for the journey through the many corridors leading to the community room, we stopped off at the social worker's office and delivered a document we had constructed which outlined Bethany's life and our perspective on her decent into illness. The social worker thanked us and commented that they never received such detailed information from families. We knew the 72-hour hold was rapidly coming to an end and we wanted the psychiatrists to have as much information as possible for the court hearing, even though we had been reassured they did not foresee much difficulty in getting the hospital stay extended.

Bethany appeared happy to see us when we arrived in the community room and seemed surprised we had brought her a piece of pie. She said it was her favorite and that she had not thought about French silk pie for many years. She was friendly and expressed her desire for my husband and me to spend time each day doing fun things during our trip even though she was still hospitalized and could not join us. She particularly wanted us to visit Disney Land. Little did she realize how much pain we had been experiencing each hour we were apart, and having any kind of fun was certainly the last thing on our minds. Since we had gained so much additional insight into her life between the afternoon and evening sessions, it was awkward knowing just what topic to introduce. It was very odd to work at rebuilding a relationship in such a dysfunctional situation and environment.

We asked Bethany about the facility and how she spent her day. She described an outdoor courtyard and said she spent some of her time outside, but mostly she stayed in her room and wanted to read her Bible. She mentioned giving her consent to be videotaped during an interview by one of the psychiatrists. It was her understanding that the recording would be used for educational purposes at the medical school. Permission had been granted for her to access a piano in the hospital basement on a limited basis, and she had been able to recall from memory a few excerpts from classical pieces and the entire theme from the movie *Forrest Gump*.

The conversation drifted toward current happenings in our lives and our home in Ohio. She had never seen our house because we had moved to a different neighborhood a few months after her return from Africa. Our move coincided with the beginning of our estrangement. We described our house, our yard, and the community in which we lived. In a tenuous and gentle manner, we extended to her an option of moving back to Ohio to live in our home. Without hesitation she rejected our offer, stating that although she might like to visit us in the future, she had no desire to move in with us on a permanent basis. She was happily focused on her own life and loved living near the university.

At the conclusion of the Monday evening visiting session, Bethany told us she wanted to see us again before our departure on Friday. She suggested meeting somewhere near the university as she fully expected to be out of the hospital the following morning. Because she did not have a phone she wondered how we would find her after being discharged. We asked for her home address and once again she became defensive and elusive. Without reaching a decision on where we would reunite the next day, we left the unit and walked across the parking lot to our car. We were physically and emotional exhausted, and we marveled when realizing it was still only Monday. It was hard to believe we had just arrived in town late Sunday morning.

TWENTY

Early Tuesday morning we awoke with an acute awareness that the 72-hour hold was about to expire. But even with this in mind, were not overly concerned about Bethany being discharged. We knew she had been diagnosed with schizophrenia and psychosis, she was presumed to be homeless, and she continued to refuse prescribed medication. It seemed to us that the combination of those factors would be enough to assure a long stay on a psychiatric unit. Also, the psychiatrists had not communicated their concern about an early discharge.

As we faced a new day, we decided to spend the morning hours in the university area. There was so much we did not know about her life, and we had come to believe her "home" had to be located somewhere near the main campus of the university.

After parking our car, we walked directly to the courtyard area across from the campus, which was adjacent to where her mailbox was located. We began talking with food vendors who were not actively engaged with customers. We asked them generic questions about homeless people who frequented the area. We discovered several of the vendors distributed free food in the evenings to homeless people, right before closing time. The more we talked, the more comfortable we became asking more specific questions.

We remembered the different types of food Bethany especially enjoyed in her youth and noticed a kiosk which specialized in Italian food. The woman behind the counter appeared to be particularly friendly. We described Bethany's physical appearance and surprisingly, the woman seemed to know her. Apparently, Bethany had requested food from this vendor on several occasions. The woman went on to explain how there had been an increase in requests for food by homeless people. On one occasion, leftovers had already been distributed when Bethany came by asking for a handout. The woman recalled an incident where Bethany had become angry with one of the other vendors when her request for a hand out was denied. She explained that the event made her feel very uncomfortable, and someone standing nearby called campus security. We thanked her for the times she had extended kindness to our daughter and offered to reimburse her generosity. She refused our money and told us she had given freely and out of compassion.

The new information we were uncovering was agonizing to process. The overload of distressing information over the last few days took a heavy toll on our minds and bodies. Somehow in a self-preserving sense, we developed the ability to deflect the full measure of emotional pain from piercing the innermost layers of our hearts. We had traveled too far, and too much was at stake to allow ourselves the luxury of falling apart. Since it seemed we had exhausted our resources in the food court, we felt the need to move on. However, I had one more stop I needed to make.

I knew there were facilities in the back of the building and felt drawn to take a look inside the ladies' restroom. As I opened the door and stepped inside, an unkempt woman was standing by the sink with dripping wet, tangled hair. Upon my entry, she hastily gathered her belongings, which included a small bottle of shampoo, and left. I was sorry to have disturbed her, and paused just long enough to look into the mirror above the sink. In my mind I saw Bethany's face reflecting back at me and I imagined how she might have used the sink just like the woman had done. The envisioned scenario was terrible to think about and I quickly retreated to rejoin my husband.

While the two of us walked to our car I explained what I had seen and imagined. Being in the food court had been difficult, but mercifully it had also brought to mind a sweet memory from a trip I had taken to visit Bethany in August 2000, just weeks before she had begun her sophomore year. Together, we had tried on dresses in one of the courtyard stores, and I had bought her a blue one. I remembered we had also purchased a comfortable pair of athletic shoes to replace the pair she had so thoroughly worn out from walking miles each day to and from her classes and the lab. The disparity between the sweet memory and our current situation was too sorrowful and vast to fully take in.

There was a bit of unscheduled time remaining before having to depart for the Tuesday afternoon visiting session, so we decided to do a little exploring just beyond the campus boundary. It was remarkable seeing the dense student population significantly diminish just one block away from campus. The surrounding neighborhood appeared to be a congestion of apartments and subdivided small homes along with a few churches and small shops. The general population appeared to be multicultural and fairly safe. However, as we continued to observe, we became increasingly aware of a persistent theme which had strong representation on the campus itself and stretched well into the outlying neighborhood. Wherever we looked, we noticed a significant number of people who appeared to be homeless. Some of them walked slowly down sidewalks wearing dirty, tattered clothing while transporting possessions in bags and shopping carts, and others sat motionless on bus stop benches, staring with vacant eyes. Despair and misery was all around us. With all of this filling our minds, we realized it was time to begin our journey back to the hospital to see Bethany.

As we merged onto the expressway we encountered the lunch hour rush and a traffic jam. The drive to the hospital was slow and tedious, causing us to be late for the visiting hour. After clearing security we anxiously joined the second wave of visitors being escorted to the community room.

As the security guard unlocked and opened the door to the unit where Bethany was staying, we saw her approaching us from a distance down a hallway. With an eager smile she waved to greet us. She was dressed in a long colorful patchwork skirt, a tan corduroy jacket, and the black sandals we purchased for her the day before. She was bright and cheerful as together we walked into the community room. When I inquired about her jacket and skirt, she said it was the outfit she had worn on the day she was brought to the hospital. She explained that her clothing had been taken by emergency room staff and held until everything could be washed. She casually mentioned that her outfit had been dirty and had smelled bad. Because everything had been returned to her, she said she no longer needed the things we brought for her. At our discretion, she was willing to donate the items to needy patients who had already shown interest, or she would return them to us. Remarkably, a few women had already been willing to accept a few things.

Bethany appeared to be quite energized and upbeat, and said she would be released from the hospital later in the day. This news forcefully threw us off guard. Her expression of excitement and relief about the imminent return to her "home" baffled us, especially in light of her presumed homelessness. Throughout the visiting session we found it extremely difficult to concentrate and converse normally with her because we desperately needed to know what was happening behind the scenes. By watching the confidence and excitement she portrayed, and feeling a growing inward panic, it was nearly impossible to remain seated.

With guarded words we asked Bethany about the life she would be returning to, and once again we requested her home address. Our direct approach seemed to make her very uncomfortable and she made a casual attempt to deflect the question. We mentioned the neighborhoods around the university and pressed her further. She responded with a quick and vague answer, but in that answer I thought I heard the word garden and something about a Thirty-Sixth Street. We were trying to extract as much information as possible without pressing too hard and causing her to shut down. While we urgently spoke with her, one of the psychiatrists came into the room and said he needed to meet with us privately. We hurriedly said goodbye to Bethany and made an attempt to assure her that, even if she left the hospital, we would somehow try to find her before flying back to Ohio on Friday.

The psychiatrist informed us that Bethany had spoken with an advocate from a human rights organization. These advocates were known to provide assistance to patients seeking early release from court ordered hospitalization. Although Bethany was not yet legally pursuing immediate discharge, the doctor explained that intervention by this organization on her behalf could make it more difficult to keep her hospitalized against her will. This new information was like a slap in the face. Immediately we realized our daughter could be back on the street in no time, having gained knowledge and experience on how to manipulate the system that had mercifully delivered her to the threshold of treatment and recovery.

The psychiatrist also informed us that Bethany had disclosed a specific house number on a Thirty-Sixth Street which she claimed to be her place of residence. He impressed upon us the urgency and importance of verifying whether or not this address was valid. When Bethany listed the address, the hospital no longer considered her homeless. This placed her in a better position to exert legal pressure if she decided to formally apply for early discharge. Not only did we have to find the address listed, but we also had to determine whether she actually lived there. If the address turned out to be false, then we had to somehow come up with reliable documentation to disprove her claim.

The psychiatrist asked if we would be willing, if necessary, to testify against Bethany in order to keep her in the hospital. We believed hospitalization was her only hope to recognize her illness, and we passionately agreed to testify. We resolved to focus every last bit of our strength toward the prevention of an early discharge. If some unknown advocate planned to argue Bethany's legal right to live a life of untreated mental illness, then we would fight against them with all our might to promote treatment, recovery, and a life full of promise.

As we left the hospital, it felt as though an hourglass had been turned upside down and the sand was just pouring out. With limited time and resources, and in a strange and crowded city, we set off to find the address. Reinvigorated with adrenaline, we hurried to our car and headed back to the university area.

We were on a desperate mission. Without delay, we had to find the address and someone willing enough to provide reliable information. We located Thirty-Sixth Street on a map and it appeared to be close to the university neighborhood we had just driven through earlier in the day, before driving to the hospital.

When we arrived in the area, we found the community to be a tightly condensed mixture of apartment buildings and small, free-standing family homes. The buildings appeared to have multiple entrances and separate addresses. Streets in the neighborhood stopped and started again at unusual angles. We would drive down one street only to discover, after traveling just a short distance that the name of the street had somehow changed.

We found Thirty-Sixth Street and began to drive very slowly in order to identify house numbers. Some buildings had different numbers on upstairs and downstairs doors, and some were posted in fractions. Others were devoid of any sort of marking.

Due to busy traffic and our slow speed, cars kept coming up behind us, causing us to circle around the block numerous times in order to figure things out. We found an address very close to what we needed, but not the exact address we were looking for. My husband stopped the car next to a line of tightly parked vehicles. When I opened the car door to get out, the scorching heat of the day consumed me.

I approached a house with an address closest to the number we were seeking, walked up the few steps to the front door and knocked. After a bit of a wait, a scruffy looking man answered the door. I asked him if he was aware of a house with the street number we had been given. I described Bethany's appearance and inquired whether he knew her or had seen her. He appeared annoyed and curtly told me he did not know of the address, and knew nothing about Bethany.

I spotted another house across the street with an address close to the address we needed. I ran to the house and knocked on the door while my husband circled around the block. It appeared to be a building with multiple apartments and I wondered if we had found the home of Bethany's friends who had invited her to spend time with them. I knocked several times and waited, but no one answered.

I got back into the car and my husband found a place on the side of the street where we could temporarily park. We were hot, sweaty, and completely defeated. In frustration and surrender, we sat together in silence. After a few minutes we bowed our heads and prayed for guidance. After this brief interlude, we drove away from Thirty-Sixth Street, not knowing what to do next.

As we headed out of the neighborhood, we turned onto a narrow and seemingly long street and continued to look at the street signs. Within just a few blocks, we spotted a sign for a Thirty-Sixth *Place.* It appeared to be an entirely different street from the one we had just left. My husband turned the car around and we anxiously looked for house numbers. The homes appeared a bit rougher and house numbers were challenging to find. But as we slowly crept forward, we began to sense a spark of hope. The numerical progression appeared to logically advance toward the place we were seeking, and then suddenly we arrived at the exact address.

We sat motionless in the car staring at an empty, weedy lot surrounded by a high chain link fence. The fence gate was secured with a heavy chain and a rusty padlock. Arriving at our journey's end brought quick realization of Bethany's deception. The frantic search was over and our objective was fulfilled. We had set out to prove our daughter's homelessness, but deep in our hearts we had nurtured a tiny hope of finding a better end to our quest. The address could have at least been a rented room or the home of a friend. Instead, it was an unkempt vacant lot where no one could possibly live.

After sitting in front of the lot for a few minutes, we slowly drove away. Our discovery was harsh and painful. In silence, we headed toward a main road which we believed would lead us out of the neighborhood. As we drove along, we passed a tiny bookstore situated next to a large church building. Suddenly I recalled Bethany mentioning something about a bookstore in one of our conversations. A narrow sidewalk ran alongside the store which seemed to continue toward the church yard. We pulled over and I quickly got out of the car to look around. As I started down the sidewalk I noticed a small teddy bear stuffed into a row of bushes. Seeing the abandoned bear made me sad as I imagined how some unknown child had apparently lost a much-loved toy.

As I continued toward the churchyard, the sidewalk sharply turned to the left and instantly delivered me into an expansive well-kept cactus garden. As I stepped into the area an acute and powerful realization washed over me and I instantly knew it was Bethany's "home." I had no doubt about it. I could feel it.

I walked around to the front of the church and climbed the large cement steps leading to the main entrance. The doors were locked. However, due to my new vantage point I was able to see there was an additional, very similar and large cactus garden located on the opposite side of the church adjacent to a grassy lawn and a strip of bushes. I also noticed a man working near the street in front of the church. He was shoveling sand into a wheelbarrow which appeared to be destined for the cactus gardens. I approached him and started asking questions. I was able to learn that at night, homeless people entered the churchyard to sleep. I described Bethany's appearance and mentioned her name. Then I introduced myself as Bethany's mother. A slow easy smile spread across the man's face and he said, "Yes, I know her, she is my friend."

The man confirmed that Bethany did indeed live in the churchyard. He said she had been doing well up until the winter months and then had begun to have problems. He was aware she had been taken away by police on Saturday and seemed relieved to know she was in the hospital. He smiled at me and said he always knew there must be a family out there somewhere who loved and missed Bethany. I asked for his name. Then I inquired if he would be willing to provide testimony confirming Bethany's homeless status if it was necessary to help assure her recovery. He casually seemed to agree and said he could usually be found near the church. Right as I was finishing up my conversation with the man, my husband walked up behind me and greeted him.

My husband had somehow managed to find a parking space and had followed the same path down the narrow sidewalk. Together we thanked the man for his information and I gave him one of my business cards, with the request to please call if he ever witnessed Bethany's return to a homelessness life. As soon as my husband and I were alone again, he described how he was hit by the same strong feelings I had just experienced upon entering the garden. He also knew instantly we had found our daughter's "home."

Before returning to our car, we paused a few moments just to experience the area. The sandy plant beds were filled with every shape and size of large succulents, a garden so familiar to Bethany, a refuge, and the place she called "home." We were overcome by emotion and grief, too affected to even cry. Assumptions regarding Bethany's homelessness had vanished. We knew we were standing right in the center of harsh and raw reality.

Although the experience in the garden hit us very hard, we were grateful to finally know the truth. As we entered rush hour traffic on our way back to the hospital, we looked for a place where we could access a computer and have a document printed. We felt an urgency to update our timeline as quickly as possible with the new information we had just discovered. It seemed that everything hinged upon our new discovery.

Along the route toward the hospital, we ran across an office supply store where we knew we could have a document printed, but we were not sure about accessing a computer. When we entered the store, we spoke to a woman behind the printing counter who explained that customers were not allowed to use company computers for word processing. When we disclosed how an updated document was needed to keep our mentally ill daughter in a psychiatric hospital, the woman decided to bend the rules. She said she could relate with our distress because she had just experienced the death of her mother. Her decision enabled my husband to complete our document and have it printed. I went out to the car to phone my sister, even though I was aware that the nightmare we were experiencing was too sensational to fully describe.

We had not eaten for hours, so we were relieved to find a restaurant next to the office supply store. It did not matter to us what kind of food the restaurant served. Food was merely the fuel that kept us going. Under such an enormous load of stress, we rarely felt hunger and had to force ourselves to eat.

Early Tuesday evening, when we arrived at the hospital for the visiting session, we headed directly to the social worker's office to submit our document. The social worker assured us the new information would help keep Bethany in the hospital.

Escorted by a security guard, we were ushered toward the community room to meet with Bethany. Although she still wore the patchwork skirt and tan jacket, she appeared less energized than she had been earlier in the day. However, she continued to talk about being released. For us, things had dramatically changed in the few hours since we had been together, and we felt we could be a bit bolder in our conversation. We believed the new information we had gathered gave us a stronger foothold in the battle to save our daughter's life.

Together, the three of us sat in a corner of the noisy community room. My husband asked Bethany a question about her finances. She said she lived a simple life and required very little money. I noticed her restlessness as she answered his question. Then she communicated an urgent desire to return to her home as soon as possible. She said she wanted to keep her life intact, just as it had been before being picked up by the police.

Bethany stated that she wanted to continue in a relationship with us and suggested we connect by phone every few weeks. The only assistance she asked from us was to help her set up an account for a new mailbox. She specified that it needed to be located away from university property. As we continued to talk with her about these things, we gained a deeper understanding of the way illness affected her thought process. She seemed blind to the reality of her broken life and truly unaware of how much she had lost. Life outside the hospital appeared to be a type of delusion for her, providing a sense of security and comfort. We were beginning to understand the extent of her separation from reality. After the visiting hour was over, somehow we got ourselves back to the hotel and into bed.

TWENTY-ONE

On Wednesday morning we woke up entirely wasted. After receiving the call from the police on Saturday we had barely stopped to breathe, sleep, or eat. We had been bombarded with more information than our minds and emotions could handle, and we were anxious about what the new day would bring.

Even though we had disproved her claim of having a valid home address, we felt compelled to uncover as much information as we could that would weigh the case against Bethany in the event we were called to testify. To this end, we decided to send emails to a few of our old contacts, to inform them of her hospitalization and to seek their help. Because they were Bethany's friends, and had expressed concern about her welfare, we thought they might be willing to write an email, or at least provide verbal information to the hospital social worker. Our efforts were promptly rewarded as one person responded and agreed to call the social worker. This same person loosely agreed to testify against Bethany if it was deemed necessary.

With only two days remaining before our departure to Ohio, things were still up in the air. The psychiatrists and hospital staff had been working with Bethany, but so far she had refused to take medication. We were kept updated on her status and had a lunchtime appointment scheduled with the psychiatrists just prior to the Wednesday afternoon visiting session.

Upon arriving at the hospital, we went through the security procedure and waited to be called into a conference room. Because it was our fourth day of visiting, the security guards were getting used to seeing us. We consistently found them friendly and encouraging.

Sometimes while waiting to be escorted to the unit, a guard would give us a verbal report on which staff members Bethany had most recently beaten at Ping-Pong. A few of the older guards appeared to be somewhat partial to her in a grandfatherly way, as they said she was an "atypical" psychiatric patient. She was well spoken, educated, and other than politely refusing treatment, she had been mostly pleasant and agreeable. In contrast, we understood the hospital admitted an overwhelming amount of people brought in after being involved in fights and issues with illegal drugs.

During our Wednesday afternoon meeting, the psychiatrists acknowledged our success in discovering the empty lot and the garden. But instead of asking further questions about what we had seen, they directed the conversation toward the broader perspective of Bethany's severe illness and homelessness. In her psychotic state, they believed she experienced the hallucination of hearing voices. This was something Bethany had continually denied. In working closely with her, they were making slow but steady progress toward her acceptance of a medication trial, but she had not yet given her consent.

The new information about Bethany's home address weighted the case against her early release from the hospital, but the psychiatrists still had concern about her involvement with the human rights advocate. They explained that even if Bethany could be held in the psychiatric unit for an extended period of time, as long as she did not recognize her illness or consent to take medication, the likelihood of her return to the street was inevitable as well as her legal right.

We had reached the bottom line. It was beyond comprehension that after so much suffering she would have come so close to treatment and simply walked away. It was horrifying to imagine her continued life on the street.

The psychiatrists said the strongest foundation Bethany could build her recovery upon was her own awareness and acceptance of her illness. It would require self-motivation to adhere to long-term treatment which was the key to regaining a healthy mind.

We left the conference room with a deeper understanding of a realistic recovery plan and a clearer vision of just where things stood. Although her release from the hospital would be temporarily blocked by the information we uncovered, she would eventually be released. Along with our deeper understanding, we also felt a heavier burden of anxiety and fear.

We could not remain on the West Coast for an extended amount of time without losing our jobs, and we could not spend the rest of our lives running after her to keep her safe. Time was running out. Somehow we needed to convince Bethany to willingly accept treatment and move to our home in Ohio. We had nothing to lose by taking a bold and hard-line approach with our daughter.

On that Wednesday afternoon, after our meeting with the psychiatrists, my husband and I were ushered into the community room. Bethany was waiting for us. Instead of the patchwork skirt, she wore a pair of jeans and a sweater. She seemed emotionally deflated and disappointed to still be in the hospital. As usual, the room was crowded and full of loud, disruptive patients. Without delay, the three of us headed into the far corner of the room.

As soon as we sat down, we told Bethany that instead of using our daily "free time" for sightseeing, we had used it to uncover information about her life. We reported how we had driven to her "home" address and found it to be a vacant lot surrounded by an impenetrable chain-link fence. With accuracy, we were able to describe the look and feel of the cactus garden. Then we told her about the conversation we held with her friend at the church, and how he readily confirmed her homelessness.

We recounted our visit with the university security officer and told her we were aware of her outstanding warrant for arrest, due to her failure to appear in court. In addition to all the alarming facts we discovered, we had also learned she had been held in jail for disturbing the peace. As we threw the fragments of her broken life at her in a rapid, non-emotional manner, she appeared to be stunned. She was incredulous that we had uncovered so much information about her private life in such a short amount of time.

Even as we exposed the raw facts of her life, she clung to the delusion of a happy, fulfilling existence. Although she communicated regret and sadness about being restricted from university property, she seemed to take it in stride, affirming her continuing desire to live life on the fringes of the campus where she was once a promising student.

We explained to Bethany that a move to Ohio would offer an opportunity for a fresh start where all her needs would be met. But as we continued to talk she blocked and countered every argument while passionately and pitifully clinging to her dangerous life. While recognizing her legal right to refuse a move to Ohio, one fact stood apart from all the others. We stressed the point that she was being held against her will as a patient in a psychiatric hospital after being handcuffed and brought in by police. She had been recognized by the community at large, and the community had made a powerful statement about her mental status.

As she continued to bargain for a return to her old life, we told her that everything would be different for her because the police were fully aware of her situation. The police, the court, and the hospital system had knowledge of her homelessness, her untreated mental illness, her outstanding warrant, and her desperate need for treatment. But she seemed to really begin to listen when we reviewed in detail how profoundly her life had deteriorated since her graduation from high school. In a frank and caring manner, we explained that even though she was unable to recognize it, illness had silently invaded and twisted her life.

Together, we had figuratively pushed her into a corner where she had no reasonable place to run. It was distasteful to talk so severely with our daughter, but we knew we were all in a high stakes situation.

We started to back off a bit and began appealing to her passion for learning, as we believed she might still have a small chance of reclaiming a dimension of academic life. We explained that treatment was the key to recovery and if she wanted to return to the university sometime in the future, she could do so, having stepped out of the shadows of illness. Then we contrasted how in her current state, she could expect a life of repeated hospitalizations and possibly additional jail time.

As we tossed her a lifeline, tentatively she began to reach for it. With gentle words, we told her how much we loved her, and pledged our devotion to her recovery with the distinct goal of returning her to a healthy independent life as soon as possible. With an attitude of surrender and cautious hope, Bethany agreed to return to Ohio and move into our home. She wanted to restart her life and restore her academic dreams. However, there was one stipulation. If she wanted to live in our home, she would have to comply with psychiatric treatment, and that included her willingness to take medication. Upon hearing this, she readily agreed to begin a course of Risperdal. It was on this day Bethany took a giant step toward a recovered life.

As soon as she made her decision, her excitement seemed to grow as she shifted her focus from life on the street to life in our home, and a chance to reconnect with extended family and friends from her past. She wondered how things would appear in Ohio after living so long on the West Coast. We explained that since it was only March, she had not yet missed the arrival of spring. It delighted her to know that she would soon be watching leaves emerge on the trees, and would be able to help me plant flowers in my garden.

At the end of the visiting hour, we reluctantly left Bethany and met with her primary psychiatrist. He was eager to know what had transpired during our visit and seemed very relieved with the turn of events. We felt fairly confident she had been sincere in her agreement to accept treatment and move to Ohio. Before we parted from her she had stated her desire to inform the psychiatrist herself that she was ready to start medication.

From the moment we received the call from police on the previous Saturday, we were thrust into total chaos. Undoubtedly we had been directed through a maze of horrors. But as we looked to transition from crisis to recovery, we soberly considered the ragged pieces of Bethany's life which somehow needed to be stitched back together. The pieces would create a design none of us had planned.

When discussing Bethany's decision and consent for treatment, the psychiatrist estimated she would be ready for discharge in less than two weeks. We knew this would barely allow enough time to work out countless details requiring our attention before returning to the psychiatric hospital with three plane tickets in hand.

On Wednesday evening we arrived at the hospital for the visiting hour and found a calmer, more subdued Bethany. The medication had significantly slowed her down and she seemed more relaxed and better able to focus on individual topics. This was in contrast to earlier meetings where her speech had been quick-paced and a bit strained. Our conversation centered on her new life in our home, the people we wanted her to meet, and places she could easily access in our community that happened to be walking distance from our house. Together we sketched out a rough draft of her life so she could better visualize what to expect. Her commitment to treatment and subdued demeanor remarkably changed the dynamic of our relationship. This allowed us to feel a bit more comfortable in her presence.

TWENTY-TWO

When we returned to the unit on Thursday for the early afternoon visit, we noticed Bethany was less focused and more energized than she had been the night before. It seemed as though the medication was not effectually calming her restless mind. The change was disturbing and put us on edge.

While mentally processing my concerns, Bethany handed me a greeting card fashioned out of woven strips of red and blue colored paper. She said she made it that morning while attending therapy group. Deeply touched by this simple gift, and overwhelmed by a rush of emotion, I embraced my twenty-five-year-old daughter.

The dynamic of our relationship was changing, and all three of us seemed to be pulling in the same direction toward a new beginning. When my husband and I reminded Bethany about our departure the following day, she asked a lot of questions about the community where we lived and about our house. We believed she was piecing together a mental image of her future.

On our way out of the hospital that afternoon, we reported our concerns to the psychiatrist about how the medication did not seem as effective as it had been the day before. The psychiatrist explained that due to the drug being slowly introduced, it had not yet reached a therapeutic maintenance level. If Bethany continued to tolerate the medication, he still expected her to be psychiatrically stable enough for hospital discharge in less than two weeks. Until then, as the dosage increased, the professional staff would observe her response to the medication and look for any obvious untoward side effects.

When we returned later in the day for the Thursday evening visiting hour, we were relieved to find Bethany more relaxed and better focused. However, we began to recognize the term "therapeutic dosage" might have a fuzzy definition. We could not forget the sleepy young man we had observed with his parents during our initial visits to the unit. Throughout the week we watched him transition out of his lethargic state and into an angry reengagement with life. Vibrant health was what we desired for our daughter, not an overmedicated existence, and certainly not a life lived in a psychotic realm of detachment and anger.

As the visiting hour drew to a close, we embraced each other for the last time. Our flight was scheduled to depart the next day, right at the beginning of the Friday afternoon visiting hour. It was hard to leave, but we promised to stay in close phone contact until we returned. Bethany assured us she would be fine.

TWENTY-THREE

Early in the afternoon on Friday, March 9, 2007 our flight took off for Cincinnati. Each mile that distanced us from Bethany's broken life took us closer to the treasured peace and privacy of our own home. Our minds were overloaded with images from a week of horrors. Stress and anguish had reached legendary levels. What we experienced went far beyond anything we could have possibly imagined.

After a very long day of travel, we pulled into our garage just before midnight. The comfort and shelter of our home and the familiarity of our former lives wrapped around us like a blanket. By just stepping through the door, our bodies began to truly relax. We were bone tired.

In little less than a week, we had each lost over five pounds. We wished we could rewind our lives back to the previous Saturday morning before the call came from the police. We preferred to envision a scenario where our healthy daughter simply decided to return home. But it did not matter what we preferred. Everything we had lived through had been real, and once again sand in the hourglass of time seemed to be pouring out.

It turned out that we would have roughly nine days before having to fly back and pick up Bethany. In that time we needed to mentally process everything, catch up in our full-time jobs, set up a bedroom and attend to a thousand other details. There was a lot involved in preparing for a smooth transition. It was tempting to imagine that by just moving her into our home she would be "okay," but we knew better. We were embarking upon an unchartered course, unable to truly understand the depth of her illness or her capacity for recovery.

After careful consideration, we made the decision to move Bethany into a bedroom with a view of the backyard flower garden, even though it required moving quite a bit of furniture and switching and condensing the contents of closets and dressers. We also decided to remove all our personal items from our spare bathroom so it would belong to her exclusively.

Throughout the week, after completing my work days, I tried to create a pleasing and welcoming environment for Bethany. I also purchased a few clothing items and some pretty bath and beauty products she could enjoy until we had a chance to shop together.

It was impossible not to recognize the stark contrast between the mountain of possessions we transported into her first dorm room, and her total lack of personal items beyond a ragged tan jacket, a patchwork skirt, and a worn-out pair of black shoes.

My husband purchased plane tickets for our return flight to the West Coast for Monday, March 19, as Bethany's discharge date had been tentatively set for Tuesday March 20. He connected with a public defender and a court date was set for Wednesday, March 21. The court date would provide an opportunity for Bethany to settle her outstanding warrant. Plane tickets were also secured for the three of us to fly back to Ohio. The itinerary allowed two full days after Bethany's discharge to tie up loose ends and head home.

It was extremely difficult to be back in town and interacting with familiar people while considering all the tender emotions we tried to suppress. On Sunday we returned to our church. Throughout our ordeal we had been able to hold our emotions in check. But because we were home, surrounded by so many friends who genuinely loved and cared for us, it was especially hard to keep ourselves together.

Even though we freely shared news about Bethany's impending move into our home, we felt it was important to establish a boundary which would protect her privacy. We chose not to share all the details of our trip, Bethany's diagnosis, or her medication. In all our actions we wanted to promote her recovery, and every day we knew we would have to earn her trust.

On Monday morning I returned to work. I stopped in at my office just long enough to make phone contact with my nursing supervisor and arrange an immediate meeting with her. We had worked together for years and had a long history of working through high profile medical issues in the lives of disabled people. After a short drive across town, I entered her office and closed the door. The raw, pent up emotion I had so tightly guarded over the previous week poured out like a waterfall. In a rush of tears and grief, I spilled out the entire story. With compassion, she offered her support while I broke into heart-wrenching sobs. I have no doubt fellow workers in the surrounding offices clearly overheard the pitiful sounds that flowed from my broken heart.

After making it through the first workday, the remainder of the short week passed in a rapid succession of blurry days. My husband and I juggled heavy workloads and a mountain of preparations for Bethany's arrival. Oddly, our week between flights coincided with previous arrangements to have our roof replaced. It was amazing how despite loud erratic hammering just above our heads, we were able to fall asleep on the couch immediately if we paused to rest longer than just a few moments.

TWENTY-FOUR

After tending to an enormous amount of details in little more than a week, on Monday afternoon, March 19, we again boarded a plane. We left home to rejoin our daughter and totally transform the dynamic of our lives. Over the years we had grown quite accustomed to living alone as empty nesters and had much to learn about incorporating an adult daughter into the rhythm of our lives. It was interesting how as family we knew each other well, but at the same time we had become strangers by being apart for so many years.

Late Monday evening we arrived at our hotel and reviewed the ambitious schedule we had constructed for ourselves. On Tuesday morning, March 20, 2007 our first activity of the day was to meet with the psychiatrists and pick up Bethany. Since she had been compliant and was tolerating a maintenance dose of medication, she was considered stable and ready for discharge. She had been hospitalized a total of 16 days. Instead of our usual routine of going through security and being led down secure hallways, we were told to wait in the lobby where a psychiatrist would join us. After we briefly spoke with a psychiatrist and a nurse, Bethany was escorted out of her unit and into our care. She appeared very relieved to see us and eager to leave the hospital.

We were given a 30-day supply of Risperdal and instructions to find a psychiatrist for follow-up care in Ohio. The hospital psychiatrist offered to consult with us by phone as needed until we were able to establish Bethany with a psychiatric physician in Ohio.

Her discharge summary mentioned homelessness, schizophrenia, cognitive impairments, and a care level requiring oversight for medication and activities of daily living. We were also given a formal document which was written and signed by one of the psychiatrists. This document described Bethany's physical appearance, her situation, and our plan to move her to Ohio. We were a bit nervous about having enough identifying information for airline security. Even though her dad had checked with the airline beforehand, we knew the individual security official at the gate could accept or reject whatever we had to offer.

We conveyed our gratitude to the psychiatrist and hospital staff for the care and compassion they extended to Bethany. Together, the three of us exited through the front door of the locked facility. While walking, I glanced up at the sign in the front of the building declaring it to be a psychiatric hospital. I silently prayed that we would never again have to enter such a place.

It was nearly noon as we wound our way through heavy traffic toward the university area, and we were hungry. When we arrived near the campus, we spotted a restaurant which was situated directly across the street from one of the main gates. It was a cook-to-order steak place with an open buffet table. We ordered steaks, grabbed trays, and headed to a table by a window facing the bustle of active students walking to and from their classes.

On our first pass through the buffet line we watched as Bethany placed an impressive amount of food on her plate. It was plain to see she was relishing the abundance. As we sat down, entered into light conversation, and began to eat, the waiter served our steaks. Our silent amusement at Bethany's zesty appetite quickly turned bittersweet as we recognized she was being served a banquet right beside her beloved university, after enduring years of exile, homelessness, and hunger.

After lunch we drove a few blocks to the university security office. Bethany and I waited in the car while her dad entered the building. During the previous week he arranged with a security officer to have the university reprint a student ID using a file photo of Bethany they still retained in their computer system. When her dad placed the photo ID card into Bethany's hand, she handled it as if it were made of pure gold because it declared her to be a valid and current student. We explained that the ID was for airline use only and when we arrived at our home in Ohio, we would have to mail it back to the university.

Our next stop was the bank. Her dad had made previous arrangements for a locksmith to drill through the lock on her safe deposit box so she could collect the contents and close her account. This procedure required a large fee and photo ID. While Bethany and I waited in the bank lobby, she recalled that it had been a very long time since she had entered the bank. After a lengthy and tedious wait the locksmith finally arrived and drilled open the box.

We watched in amazement as Bethany completely filled a briefcase with documents she had so carefully protected, despite her homelessness. We understood these valued papers to be records for her non-profit organization and pages of an independent self-study project she engaged in after dropping out of school. In the box, she also found her passport. It was filled with colorful stamps from countries all over the world, including China, Thailand, England, Kenya, Nigeria, Myanmar and Taiwan. After the closure of her account, she reclaimed a few hundred dollars in cash which amazingly, she had tucked away in case of emergency. As we left the bank, all our business commitments were completed for the day. We drove away from the university area and toward the community where our hotel was located.

We had not expected the weather to suddenly turn chilly, as it had been remarkably warm during our previous trip. Since Bethany appeared to be cold, we stopped off at a department store. I helped her pick out a sweater and coaxed her toward the jewelry counter. We encouraged her to choose a pair of earrings, as we noticed she no longer possessed any type of jewelry. She was very timid in her selection as she was clearly no longer accustomed to being treated special, even in this small way. Eventually she settled on a pair of white enamel earrings imprinted with tiny blue flowers.

Throughout the day as her dad and I confidently transitioned from place to place, we noticed Bethany seemed to lag behind us, somewhat hesitant and guarded, especially while walking through entrances, approaching counters, and accompanying me into public restrooms. Her demeanor portrayed a shy uncertainty of acceptance. It was apparent her homeless lifestyle had pushed her toward the shadowed edges of society. Her former appearance in any setting must have automatically triggered close scrutiny by others at every turn.

In gathering and putting on the little pieces of normal life such as the sweater and earrings, we sensed a tiny sprout of confidence beginning to emerge in Bethany, even though the community at large seemed to intimidate her.

Our hotel was located in an upscale part of town where we spent time with Bethany in previous years, so we knew she was fairly familiar with the area. As we drove along we found a multileveled outdoor mall where we believed we could enjoy a bit of walking exercise while doing a bit of window-shopping. As we began exploring, we approached a large, open area in front of a movie theater entrance. Bethany suddenly stopped and in a sort of reverent realization, explained that she was standing on the very spot where on one of her birthdays, friends had gathered to surprise her with a party. The place we had unexpectedly stumbled upon held sweet and treasured memories of her past life when she had been connected to friends and had felt valued.

As the three of us continued to explore and window shop in the large mall area, we found a trendy, upscale department store with a fine jewelry counter. Bethany appeared interested in looking but seemed hesitant to get close enough to really see what was displayed in the cases. I stepped next to her and quietly encouraged her to walk closer, and told her she had every right to look at the beautiful rings and necklaces just like the other shoppers.

Evening was approaching and it had been many hours since our lunch, so we decided to find a place to buy a light supper. We spotted a casual little sandwich shop advertising soup and salad. As we picked out a table, Bethany objected to spending additional money for food since we had already eaten in the university area earlier in the day. We said we wanted to have another meal because so many hours had passed since lunch, and then after eating, we would head to the hotel for the remainder of the night. She said she was uncomfortable ordering food twice in one day, and with the necessity of having to rely on us to pay for her every time. We talked about her concerns and said it was our pleasure to buy food for her, but she would only agree to order the cheapest and smallest cup of soup on the menu. When our meals arrived we found it fascinating as she supplemented her austere choice with a variety of free complementary side items such as crackers and croutons offered by the restaurant.

After such a long day I was grateful when we pulled up in front of our hotel. We were all tired and settled into a room with two queen sized beds, one for her and one for us. After accepting responsibility for her we had no intention of letting her out of our sight until we arrived safely in our own home in Ohio.

TWENTY-FIVE

When we woke up on Wednesday morning we could sense Bethany's anxiety. We had two important agenda items planned for the day. A court hearing was scheduled in the morning and we had a 10:21 PM flight scheduled which would take the three of us back to Ohio.

In preparation for this day, I had packed a tailored skirt and jacket for Bethany to wear during her court appearance. Although she was well-dressed, to me, she looked nervous and vulnerable. I was worried about how she would hold up in front of a judge. I tried to calm my fears by knowing, that as keeper of the medicine bottle, I had seen her take every dose of prescribed medication right on time. Her dad and I reminded her that we would be right beside her every step of the way, and that a public defender familiar with her case would be representing her. As we drove toward the courthouse, I was surprised by the considerable span of miles which separated the congested downtown and the university area. It was challenging to find the actual courthouse address because buildings were tightly packed together and pedestrian traffic was fast-paced and heavy. It would have been challenging for Bethany to find the building by herself.

We parked the car, entered the building and proceeded through a complicated series of elevators and hallways. Eventually we found the courtroom and were instructed to wait outside the door until Bethany's name was called. The place was very busy with a steady flow of people streaming through the halls.

Courtroom doors opened and closed as lists of names were loudly announced. Right when Bethany's name was being called, the public defender finally arrived. She hurriedly took Bethany and her dad aside to talk while I scanned the crowded room to find a place where the three of us could squeeze in together on one of the polished wooden benches.

As proceedings began, I could not help but notice the eclectic mix of people surrounding us on all sides. Some were dressed in odd and provocative clothing. Some appeared quite angry and possibly under the influence of alcohol or drugs. Others seemed to be small groups of family members.

As cases were presented it became clear to see that Bethany would be looked upon as just another social menace, like the prostitutes and drug users who seemed to be strongly represented in the courtroom. We watched with interest while many of them sported brazen, angry, and often flagrantly disrespectful attitudes throughout their interactions with the judge.

Bethany looked very timid when it was her turn to approach the bench, even though her dad and the public defender walked beside her. A quick, private, conversation took place between the public defender, the prosecutor and the judge, and then the judge turned to Bethany. With a stern and accusing voice, she scolded her for trespassing on university property and failing to appear in court when summoned. Then she belittled her for being a menace to such an outstanding university. She said the university did not want her on their property.

Then the judge directed her scolding at my husband, verbally portraying "Bethany's parents" as irresponsible, indulgent people who fostered her menacing behavior. Then she asked for Bethany's verbal agreement to never return to the university. Bethany agreed.

Due to Bethany's financial status, court fees were dismissed. But she was branded with a misdemeanor charge for disturbing the peace. The situation was tragic. Cruel admonishment had been directed toward a young woman who lost her academic dreams, suffered in homelessness, and only that morning completed a 16-day hospitalization in a psychiatric ward. Somehow, Bethany bore it all bravely.

The minute we were dismissed, we left the courtroom and tried to shake off the guilt and shame. It was tremendously freeing to walk away having completed the last big hurdle of our trip. As we approached our rental car in the parking garage we had one common purpose. We wanted to find a beach where we could grab lunch and spend the remainder of the day unwinding before embarking upon our long trip back to Ohio later that evening.

Slowly, we wove our way out of the city traffic toward the long, expansive coast. After a lengthy, scenic drive we stopped for lunch. Bethany was talkative, recalling a time when she and a friend ate together at the very same restaurant. When we were done eating, we found a narrow, desolate stretch of beach where we could walk and experience the waves and the sand.

The ocean environment brought back memories of family vacations when our children were young. This sparked conversation, mentally transporting us to a time when life had been innocent and hopes and dreams had stretched before us. Back then, we could not have imagined such a future lay ahead for our daughter and for us.

As we slowly made our way down the beach, sticky coarse sand coated our bare feet and occasionally, chilly waves washed over our legs, catching us by surprise. The wind was strong, and seagulls circled around us looking for food.

After a while, Bethany seemed to become fatigued and disengaged, so while my husband continued onward to do a bit more exploring, Bethany and I sat together on a big log that protruded out from a pile of tumbled driftwood. She was quiet and appeared to be deep in thought. Truthfully, I was tired too. The morning had been tremendously stressful and nothing short of a nightmare. Throughout the previous weeks, both her dad and I mentioned to each other that our hearts literally hurt from the monumental stress we were under.

As Bethany and I sat quietly on the piece of driftwood, my mind replayed depressing thoughts about how far we had fallen as a family. I was emotionally spent and struggled to introduce new topics I could discuss with Bethany.

Silence between us grew as I began to focus my attention on the curious shapes of driftwood scattered all around us. Then, to my amazement, I realized we were sitting perilously close to a dead brown sea lion that had blended in with the wood. Remembering Bethany's tenderness for animals, I quickly suggested that we continue walking down the beach because I did not want her to see it. After a little while, her dad rejoined us.

Looking into the distance, Bethany spotted some large patches of deep green foliage. The plants were located in an area of dry sand that skirted a series of volleyball courts. She wanted to look at the plants up close, so together we headed in that direction.

As we approached the low-growing plants, Bethany crouched down and tenderly caressed the tiny leaves with her fingers. She commented on the intricate beauty of each leaf. The plants did not appear particularly special to us but we respected her right to enjoy them. She stayed in her crouched position for quite a while, continuing to look at them very closely. Then she stood up and said she wanted to look at a few more outlying clusters of the little plants. All the foliage appeared identical to us, but we followed her and waited while she continued to examine individual leaves.

While this was going on, her dad decided to make the long trek back to the car. He said he would pick us up. He figured this plan would allow Bethany enough time to finish looking at the plants. It was hot outside and the wind had become quite strong. I continued to follow her across the beach as she repeated the process of crouching down at each cluster and examining individual leaves.

Enough time had passed where I was beginning to anticipate my husband's arrival with the car. As I watched him drive by in order to circle around, I gently coaxed Bethany to leave the plants. She was reluctant to leave the beach but agreed to join me. As we headed toward the road, we stepped onto a short sidewalk which led to a row of small homes.

There were no parking spaces and a lot of traffic. Her dad pulled the car next to the far end of the sidewalk in hope that we could reach him before traffic built up and forced him to circle around the block a second time. I realized the importance of reaching him quickly, and encouraged Bethany to hurry. She walked slowly and seemed to be in a daze. I encouraged her to speed up but she seemed physically unable to move faster. I saw my husband in the distance eagerly waiting for us, but nothing I could do or say would persuade her to speed up.

Eventually we reached the car. I was sweaty and frustrated, and her dad could not understand why it had taken us so long to walk a relatively short distance. From what he had seen, there had been no logical reason for the delay. I was irritated and the whole episode with the plants made me feel uneasy.

We spent the remainder of the long afternoon sightseeing along the coast. Bethany seemed tired, but after a short ride in the car she seemed to brighten up. There was a marine museum located on one of the long piers, so we spent time looking at fish and all sorts of sea creatures. Before the sun was fully set we headed toward the airport as we wanted to allow plenty of time for heavy traffic and long lines at the security gate.

As we approached the busy airport we began to feel the full effect of the long and stressful day. The episode with the plants had put us on edge. We knew our defenses were severely worn down. But when security cleared us without a hitch, we breathed a sigh of relief knowing we had reached the final lap of our journey.

Bethany was excited to be on a plane again because she loved flying. But she also described a deep sadness in her heart to be leaving a place she loved and considered "home" for eight years. As the plane took off, the city lights spread out below us. My mind drifted back to the time we had flown over that same city, not knowing how our daughter lived. I knew some day we would eventually have to reconcile the events of the past. Although Bethany willingly sat beside us, we could not help but feel insecure. It was clear we had not yet entirely grasped the depth of our situation or the scope of our daughter's illness.

After flying several hours, we landed in Atlanta for a rather lengthy layover before boarding our flight to Cincinnati. It was the middle of the night and the airport was quiet and almost deserted. We were sleep deprived and the combination of fatigue and stress was affecting our thinking. About an hour into the layover, as we sat on horribly uncomfortable chairs, I had the sudden realization that my little purse was missing. I had been careful to keep it tightly strapped around my waist ever since leaving the hospital, but I had become uncomfortable during the flight and unfastened it. With a surge of dread I realized that in losing my purse, I also lost Bethany's medicine. With frantic, blind panic, I ran to the first airline employee I saw in order to find out how I could retrieve it. The man explained that all abandoned items were directly sent to the Lost and Found Department, but it was closed for the night. The department would not reopen until well after our connecting flight took off. In desperation, I ran down the terminal toward the gate where we had exited the plane.

I knew the chance of recovering my purse was nearly impossible. It not only contained the bottle of medicine but also all my credit cards and over a hundred dollars in cash. When I reached the gate, the area was deserted except for one security guard, but the plane was still parked at the gate. The security guard explained that the plane had already been cleaned, and refused to let me onboard for a final look. I was grateful when he agreed to enter it himself and check where I had been seated. When he returned empty-handed, I thanked him.

In utter despair I turned around to leave. And just as I turned, I noticed two items stashed behind a counter. One of the items was my purse, intact with nothing missing. As I held the medicine bottle in my hands, a wave of relief washed over me. My mind was able to cancel out the projected scenario of landing in Cincinnati without Bethany's medicine, without a local psychiatrist, and the nightmare of losing all my credit cards. The enormity of what had almost happened made me feel weak. I had to sit down. I bowed my head and gave thanks for being granted such amazing protection. Then, without further delay, I pulled myself together and returned to our gate. I could not let Bethany see how emotionally fragile I had become.

Our plane touched down at 11 AM, Ohio time. It had been 26 hours since we had slept in a bed. Mercifully, Bethany had been able to sleep during the flights, but there was no way my husband and I could actually fall asleep. There was still too much adrenaline flowing from the stressful day.

In the Cincinnati airport, we collected our luggage and met a family friend who had offered to drive us home. We were so tired it was hard to even think. The new day was grey and rainy, and the gloomy weather stood in stark contrast to the hot sunny day we left behind just hours before. It had been over six years since Bethany experienced spring in Ohio. We realized for her, it was like entering a different world.

TWENTY-SIX

When we arrived home we gave Bethany a quick tour of our house. We were especially eager to let her see her new bedroom. She seemed pleased enough with her new environment. Although we were very tired we chose not to go directly to bed. We wanted to stay awake until at least early evening so we could better adjust to the time zone.

We settled into the family room couches and at Bethany's request, her dad started a fire in the fireplace. The afternoon was spent sitting by the fire and reminiscing. Bethany wrapped herself in a blanket and seemed content in the cozy and warm room. After several hours we finally went to bed. Bethany decided to remain on the couch and rest a while longer before retiring to her new bedroom. At different times throughout the night we heard her walking around the house. This made us both feel uneasy.

Our first few days together in Ohio were a blended mix of people and places. Bethany accompanied us to church on Sunday and was warmly and lovingly accepted. She received several invitations for dinner and other outings from some of our closest friends for the following weeks.

I scheduled a few extra days off from my nursing job so Bethany and I could spend time together shopping for the many things she needed. While familiarizing her with our community, I helped her get a state ID and a library card. She was quick to see that there were many places she could independently access within an ambitious walking distance of our home. The places included the village square which encompassed many shops, the public library, and a church. I showed her that my work office was only a few blocks from the village square.

Bethany seemed energized while picking out clothing, shoes and other personal items from many different stores. She had become much more relaxed going in and out of places than she had been on her first day out of the hospital. But even though she seemed more at ease in the community, I sensed she was not settling into her new bedroom. I had hoped that after choosing new personal belongings, she would integrate them into her room and feel more at home. In an effort to blend the past and present, we also spent time looking through stored items she had packed away from her youth.

During those first few days, she spent time on the phone with several extended family members. A few of them sent her generous gifts of money and clothing through the mail. It gave us pleasure to see her reconnect with people that loved her. It was an emotional and bittersweet time of restoration. Several times I paused to capture her picture with our camera. I was grateful that once again she would be included in our family album.

Bethany seemed to enjoy our community and especially liked the public library. When we shopped together for food, I encouraged her to choose whatever she wanted to eat. But despite my urging, she was very reluctant and conservative about adding anything to my cart. She became nervous if I appeared to purchase more than just basic necessities. Beyond our initial clothing purchases, she seemed most comfortable when I tightly regulated my spending, especially in regard to buying food.

While I concentrated on getting Bethany established in her new surroundings, her dad focused his spare time on the financial and legal areas of her life. He wrote to creditors in an effort to gain a full understanding of her indebtedness. Fortunately, she had given him free reign over the stack of mail we brought home with us.

During quiet times we noticed an underlying restlessness growing in Bethany. Quite often she mentioned how much she missed the church cactus garden where she slept during her last homeless year. Since we were experiencing unusually warm weather for March, she spent quite a bit of time in our backyard flower garden touching the tiny leaves and buds which were sprouting on the perennial plants. She said that observing and touching plants gave her a calm feeling when she felt stressed, and also helped to focus her thoughts. From inside the house we watched as she slowly bent down to carefully observe and touch the plants, just like she had done on the beach.

It was clear to us that green plants were very important to Bethany. We recognized her special fondness for cactuses and took her shopping so she could select a few for her bedroom. She also took a special interest in looking through our family room window where we had a close-up view of a tree branch where a robin was busily constructing a nest.

Both my husband and I planned one-on-one time with Bethany to work toward the rebuilding of our individual relationships. Time had changed each one of us during our long estrangement. We had entered new chapters of life. It was impossible to just pick up where we left off prior to our separation. We needed to learn how to relate to each other on an adult level. Much of our conversation centered on the topic of Bethany's future, her treatment, and her recovery. We did not know how the loose pieces of her life would come together but we believed she would regain a life of purpose and complete independence.

Because we had only a 30-day supply of medication, it was important to quickly find a local psychiatrist. We learned that most community mental health agencies only contracted with psychiatrists for a few days each month. Because of this we realized it was going to be challenging to obtain an appointment.

We found it especially difficult to find a psychiatrist with openings for new Medicaid patients. We expected that Bethany would apply for Ohio Medicaid because she had no source of personal income. The responsibility of assuming the full cost of her psychiatry appointments and her very expensive medication was far beyond our comfort zone. We had already suffered a significant financial setback with the cost of unexpected plane tickets, hotel bills, and all the things she needed to restart her life. Due to Bethany's age and the absence of any previous medical records documenting mental illness, there was no option for her to be covered under our own medical plan.

I was running into major obstacles in finding a psychiatrist and realized it could take months to get an appointment. I had no choice but to find a family practice physician willing to temporarily refill Bethany's prescription. Gratefully, I obtained an appointment with a professional colleague just days after our return to Ohio and before having to resume my full-time work schedule.

The family practice receptionist squeezed Bethany into the doctor's very tight schedule. Due to the heavy patient load, the two of us sat next to each other in his waiting room for over three hours. The wait was unbelievably long and boring. While I kept myself busy with a variety of magazine articles, Bethany sat quietly, appearing deep in thought. As time slowly crept by, I would occasionally point out a short or amusing passage I thought she would enjoy. But when I did this she would politely take the magazine and look only at the pictures. After a while I began to suspect that for some reason she preferred not to read text.

It was a relief when her name was finally called. Bethany asked me to accompany her into the examining room, as she was not familiar with the doctor. During the cursory physical exam, she revealed very little information about herself, her diagnosis, and her recent hospitalization. I struggled to remain quiet, knowing the doctor was not getting the full picture. But remembering my daughter was a twenty-five-year-old adult, I felt I needed to respect her right to interact with the doctor without my interference.

Throughout the entire appointment, Bethany was ambiguous about her need for medication. But in the end, she was handed a prescription that would continue her Risperdal. I quickly realized that the doctor had gleaned enough information to confidently write the prescription. As we left the building, I was grateful for the professional favor.

Later that day, while relaxing together in our living room, my husband and I explained to Bethany that she needed to apply for medical and disability benefits. Without pause, she rejected the idea. She made it clear to us that she had no intention of accepting money allocated for people who lacked the ability to support themselves. When we pointed out the cost of her medication and the fact that she had no resources, she strengthened her resolve. When we mentioned her agreement to take medication while living with us, the conversation swiftly disintegrated into a frustrating, circular debate.

Most of her cash supply had been spent on paying the locksmith at the bank. Even so, she demonstrated little concern about money and the financial burden her unusual situation placed upon us. Her extreme resistance to apply for benefits left us feeling frustrated and trapped. We could not understand why she so rigidly refused such a logical and reasonable request.

We decided to drop the subject for a few days. We were aggravated by the fact that her refusal not only impacted our finances, but also our entire future.

Right alongside our discussion about benefits, we began to hear Bethany mention how much she missed her "home," and how much joy it had brought her to live near the university campus. Even though she loved us, she said she considered herself to be a visitor in our home and intended to move back to the university area. One evening she asked if I would fly back with her so I could "share her joy" by visiting the places she missed and loved. My husband and I found this type of talk very disturbing. She also began engaging us in circular debates about her illness and her need for medication.

With each passing day, Bethany's desire to move back to the university area grew stronger. Her refusal to file for medical benefits, coupled with her continuing conversation about moving out, was quickly wearing us down. She was affecting us on a raw, emotional level. It was unimaginable that after all she had been through she would even consider returning to a homeless life. We were grateful to have her safely under our roof again, yet at the same time we feared she would walk out the door and we would never see her again.

The decision to remain in our home was completely in her control, just like consenting to take medication and choosing to refuse benefits. She was either going to commit to her own recovery and stay, or she would eventually leave despite our good intentions and willingness to help her.

The tension in our home was rapidly mounting and we felt pressed into taking a firm stand. With resolve, we told Bethany that if she wanted to return to the West Coast, she was free to leave at any time. However, if she made the decision to leave, we said we would no longer offer her our assistance in any way. She would have to find her own ride to the airport and come up with her own funding to pay for plane tickets and transportation back to the university area. By posturing ourselves in such a concrete way, we effectively shut down conversation on the topic. After thoughtfully considering our stand for a just few minutes, Bethany backed down. She told us she wanted to stay in our home.

Right on the heels of Bethany's renewed decision to stay, we felt compelled to confront her about her medication. My husband and I suspected that she was not being fully compliant with her treatment, even though she seemed to access her medicine bottle in the kitchen cabinet at the appropriate times. When directly confronted, she hesitantly confessed that she stopped taking the medication shortly after her arrival in our home. Her confession helped us identify the source of her increasing restlessness. Suddenly it made sense to us why she seemed to be awake at times throughout the night.

We reminded Bethany of the agreement we made requiring her to comply with treatment if she wanted to live in our home. Then we quickly realized that we had been cornered like a king in checkmate. She knew we would not turn her out of our home, and at the same time she cited the legal fact that we could not force her to take medication against her will. We found ourselves in a seemingly powerless position.

Approximately one week after returning home with Bethany, we received a follow-up call from the hospital psychiatrist. When we reported to him that she had stopped taking her medication, he estimated that it would be only a few weeks before she landed back in the hospital. It was a terrible prediction to hear. A threatening, unknown string of events loomed before us as we considered our position of responsibility and commitment to our daughter.

As we moved beyond the initial days of her return, I hesitantly settled back into to my nursing position. I found by resuming the familiar job I loved, it provided an anchor against the increasingly turbulent life we were experiencing at home. It made sense to continue working for as long as I could. My income and benefits needed to be preserved for as long as possible because the future was becoming increasingly more uncertain.

Bethany said she would feel trapped if she stayed home alone while both of us worked, so initially she decided to spend time each day working on an independent study project in the public library, teaching herself Greek and Spanish.

Because the weather continued to be unseasonably warm, she was able to independently and comfortably access our community. In the mornings, I dropped her off at the library on my way to work.

Around noon, as my schedule permitted, she walked about a half-mile from the library to my office so we could visit together and have a quick lunch.

My supervisors and coworkers were very accepting of Bethany and offered both of us an amazing amount of moral support. At the conclusion of each lunchtime visit, I escorted her out of the building and paused by the window where she could not see me. I stood silently, watching my small, gentle daughter walk away with a backpack full of books slung over her shoulder. My heart broke each time, as I recalled her shattered dreams, and my mind transposed her into the university setting where I saw her wandering aimlessly and totally alone. We were deeply grateful for Bethany's return, but at times the emotional pain was overwhelming.

During days when her dad's schedule allowed it, Bethany accompanied him on the six-mile drive to his office. She enjoyed hiking on a paved trail in a nearby Metro park which encircled a little lake where she watched the ducks. At other times she played the grand piano in our church sanctuary. She also spent time playing a student violin from her grammar school years that we had retained in our home along with several boxes of childhood memorabilia. On some days she was able to access more interesting parts of Cincinnati as several of our friends treated her to lunch and other activities. She had a lot of energy and with every passing day, her restlessness intensified along with a growing dissatisfaction with her life.

Bethany always went to bed after us, and sometimes we heard her up throughout the night. We could not help but wonder how much her intake of caffeine was affecting her sleep. She spent very little time in her bedroom and often her bed appeared as though it had barely been slept in. When she initially moved into our home, she spent a few nights sleeping on the living room couch. When we refused to let her use the living room like a bedroom, she became drawn to the bed in our finished basement.

Her preference for the basement coincided with a decreasing interest in accessing the community during our workdays. She began to spend more and more time in our home alone, waiting for us to return from our jobs so we could do things together like going to the park and taking long walks. One thing was clear. She was not happy.

Our concern was growing as it looked as though her preference for the basement was mirroring a withdrawal from the world.

TWENTY-SEVEN

March disappeared and we all looked forward to an early Easter. With the arrival of April, the weather suddenly turned bitterly cold and heavy rain turned into an ice storm. The robin outside our window abandoned her nest. The turbulent weather outside seemed to reflect the atmosphere inside our home. Despite our best efforts, we watched Bethany's life slowly spin out of control.

The spiraling restlessness which was taking her down was taking us down as well. As days passed, hopelessness grew. The fragile rays of happiness and hope we had so lovingly nurtured in our first days together were being snuffed out by a cloud of despair which hung over our home. We envisioned the years as they stretched before us, and wondered how we would ever survive.

Near the village square, and in the half-mile stretch between my office and the public library, Bethany discovered a church with beautiful stained glass windows. On the days she still spent in the community, she preferred to sit in the church sanctuary processing her thoughts. The church also had an outdoor garden with places to sit for prayer and reflection.

Bethany said she was grieving over Africa, and carried an enormous amount of guilt from the poverty and suffering she witnessed. She expressed sorrow for not being able to do more for the people she left behind. With passion, she openly shared how the contrast between rich and poor continued to torment her. She could not reconcile her current life with the impoverished people she had seen. The intensity of this unresolved conflict seemed to grow with each passing day. During our workdays she began to manage her grief by increasing the time spent at the church by my work office. She appeared to find solace by sitting silently in the outdoor prayer garden, and inside the church where she could stare at the scenes depicted in the stained glass windows.

During the Easter season we looked forward to attending a presentation of Handel's *Messiah*. This event was typically held on the Saturday evening before Easter at our own church. The choir performed this music with a full professional orchestra accompaniment and professional soloists. It was a special annual event and just the type of music Bethany loved, so we looked forward to having her accompany us.

On the day of the performance, in the late afternoon, Bethany voiced an urgent desire to spend extra time at the church near the building where I worked. We found this request to be a bit unusual for a Saturday, as she usually preferred to spend her time with us when we were not at work. She appeared restless, and explained that she would not be able to attend the concert with us unless she spent time quietly looking at the stained glass windows. At her request, I drove her to the church which was roughly a mile and a half from our home. When we arrived, she found the building closed and her restlessness increased. In desperation, I drove her to a different church several miles down the road which I believed would have a sanctuary with stained glass windows. But when we arrived, the parking lot was empty and all the doors were locked.

Because I was not aware of another church in the area which might have elaborate stained glass windows, Bethany directed me to return to the church near my office where we had just come from. At this point it was obvious to me that we would find most churches closed and locked on a Saturday afternoon. However, I was willing to make one more pass by the church near my office. When we arrived we spotted a couple of cars in the parking lot and someone walking through the front entrance. This seemed to indicate that the church had just been opened. I sensed Bethany's relief as she got out of the car.

Together we agreed that I would return to pick her up at a designated time. This arrangement would allow us to drive the six miles to the *Messiah* performance and arrive on time. Also, since she carried a cell phone, I knew she could call if she wished to be picked up earlier. As I drove away, I felt tremendous relief at being temporarily released from her restless pursuit and the pressure she had placed upon me.

When I returned an hour or so later at the agreed upon time, I found the church parking lot empty and saw Bethany sitting alone in the outdoor prayer garden. It was windy and becoming quite cold. I honked the car horn to get her attention and motioned for her to get into the car. After slowly walking over to where I was parked, she said she needed a bit more time to finish processing her thoughts. I sat in the car waiting while she returned to the garden and once again sat motionless in the cold wind, just staring.

About fifteen minutes later, I realized there was barely enough time remaining to get to the concert on time. I got out of the car and walked toward where she was sitting. Right before I reached her, a car pulled into the parking lot. Together we watched a person get out of the car, walk over to the church, unlock the main entrance and turn on the lights. Then additional cars pulled into the parking lot. The church appeared to be once again open. Upon seeing this, Bethany made a quick decision to skip the concert so she could spend additional time inside the church looking at the stained glass windows. With little time to spare, I told her that I would return in about an hour and a half to pick her up. It was getting dark, the weather had become quite cold, and I did not want her walking home alone.

Arriving late to the performance, my husband noticed Bethany was not with me. I briefly summarized what had happened. I felt anxious even though I had my phone on vibrate just in case she decided to call me. A little over an hour later without hearing from her, I hurriedly left to pick her up. When I arrived, the parking lot was empty and she was nowhere to be seen. I walked over to the church and found the doors locked. I circled around to the garden and scanned the surrounding area. She was not there. It was dark outside and I struggled to suppress my growing panic. I called her phone and she did not answer. Then I paused to remind myself that she was an adult, not a child. I headed home, hoping she would call me.

During my drive home, I half expected a call to inform me where to pick her up, but my phone was silent. When I walked through the door of our home I felt great relief to find her there in the house. She explained that not long after I left for the concert, the church had again been closed up. Instead of calling me, she walked the mile and a half distance back to our house in darkness, and against biting wind. Her hands and ears were still red and quite cold, but the physical exertion of the walk seemed to have calmed her restlessness.

As we entered the second week of April 2007, our lives were in fast motion as we tried to counteract Bethany's growing restlessness by engaging her in a variety of community activities. In the evenings, although our jobs wore us out, my husband and I took turns taking her places. On some nights we went out together as a family. Each evening our goal was to help her burn off as much physical energy as possible. We were left with very little time to relax and to be alone. Tension escalated in our home and in all of our relationships.

One evening after work, Bethany accompanied me to the grocery store to pick out snacks for a picnic. As we got out of the car and walked together toward the store entrance, I suddenly realized she was no longer walking next to me. I turned around and saw her heading back to the car. When I caught up with her she said she preferred to go to the library. I told her I would drop her off at the library as soon as we finished in the grocery store. This plan seemed to satisfy her.

Once again we started off together toward the store entrance, and again she turned around and headed back to the car. I almost had to run to catch up with her. She voiced her frustration at having left her purse at home and explained that since she did not have her purse, she did not have her library card. I told her I had my card with me and she was welcome to use it. When the third attempt to enter the store failed, out of frustration, I decided we both needed to just go home.

Bethany was in crisis. It had been several weeks since she stopped taking her medication. We could sense that she was not only grieving over Africa, but also over devastating loss in every area of her life. She mourned her inability to finish college. She was restless and unable to concentrate enough to hold even a simple part-time job. Every time she picked up her childhood violin to play, it brought sadness, as it reminded her of how she forfeited her precious lifetime instrument. The dealer to whom she sold it must have known there was something seriously wrong with her, because no one in their right mind would have parted with such a valuable violin for the shamefully small amount of money she claimed to have received.

TWENTY-EIGHT

On a Wednesday in the middle of April 2007 Bethany accompanied her dad to work for the day. Early in the afternoon she joined him while he made a few quick stops around town. One of the destinations was a music store where she planned to purchase a specific piece of music for her violin. During the drive her dad casually reintroduced the topic of applying for medical benefits.

Only one month had passed since bringing her into our home. We were on edge, and deeply affected by her restlessness. Her refusal to comply with medication was wearing us down. When her dad mentioned her finances, even though the car was still moving, she reached over and began to open the door. Her impulsive response stunned him. Immediately, he pulled the car to the side of the road and confronted her about her dangerous response. After a short and emotional interchange, he turned the car around and they headed back to his office.

Once back at the church, Bethany retreated into the sanctuary and began to play her violin. Her dad avoided that room, attending to different tasks in his office and around the building. After a while, while walking past the entrance to the sanctuary, he noticed Bethany standing motionless by the piano. As he entered the room he noticed the violin lying at her feet. Finding this behavior very odd, he picked up the violin. When he handed it back to her, he noticed that her expression was utterly blank. Her arms appeared limp as she hesitantly took the instrument from him. Just a minute after returning to his office, he heard the sound of tortured, high-pitched screaming—it was Bethany. The noise rapidly intensified as she appeared in the doorway of his office. He asked what was wrong. She stopped screaming just long enough to tell him that anyone would feel the need to scream if they had just broken a treasured violin.

Together they walked back to the sanctuary and found the violin lying in pieces on the floor. Bethany was extremely distraught and continued to scream. Very quickly he realized the situation had spun out of control. A church staff member called 911 and requested emergency medical services while my husband called me at work. When he urgently described the situation, I could hear frustrated screaming in the background. I told him I would be there as soon as I could. It took about fifteen minutes to reach the church, and during the drive I remembered the hospital psychiatrist's prediction just weeks before when we informed him of Bethany's refusal to take medication. It had not taken long for her to descend into an intolerable state of misery.

Arriving at the church, I spotted an ambulance next to the rear entrance along with a squad car. The scene hit me in a cruel and stark way as I realized the emergency vehicles were there to manage *our crisis*. Not just the crisis of our daughter's life, but the crisis of our own lives as well. Somehow, we had become one of "those families" who just cannot seem to manage on their own. Our nightmare had just spread into the community, and I knew we no longer had the physical and emotional reserve to handle it. Once again, in an act of self-preservation, we had to emotionally separate ourselves from feeling the full impact of the situation.

Stepping into the building, I found my husband and a police officer caught up in a circular debate with Bethany. It centered on her refusal to take medication and her immediate need for psychiatric intervention. She was no longer screaming, but appeared to be emotionally fragile and shaken. The officer and my husband were attempting to persuade her to get into the ambulance under her own free will, but she was flatly refusing. While sitting on a bench just inside the doorway of the building, she appeared to be struggling to control her emotions while trying to talk her way out of an overwhelmingly stressful situation.

I asked her to tell me what had happened. With an expression of deep sorrow she told me she broke her childhood violin, and then she begged me to take her home. I firmly rejected her request, explaining that we were physically exhausted and unable to continue watching her life spin out of control because she refused to take medication. In a desperate attempt, she promised to take medication if we would only take her home. My husband and I paused to look at each other and then decisively refused her request. We told her she was sick and needed to be in the hospital.

Although the police officer recognized Bethany's psychiatric instability, he said he could not legally transport her to a hospital against her will unless she posed a danger to herself or others. He explained that breaking an instrument and screaming did not meet those guidelines. When my husband pointed out her attempt to exit a moving vehicle, the officer recognized the action as a dangerous risk to self and others and agreed that she needed to be transported to the hospital.

Upon hearing this, Bethany tried even harder to bargain her way out of the situation. She was desperate to go home, but the decision had been made. With sensitivity and respect, the officer asked Bethany to get into the ambulance. He said he preferred not to use handcuffs, but would if he needed to. The statement about the handcuffs seemed to frighten her, but she refused to yield and continued bargaining for us to take her home.

Because we were living in an impossible situation, and because we loved her, we encouraged the officer to go ahead and use the cuffs. We had reached a breaking point and could not continue the stressful and exhausting life we were living. When Bethany heard us tell the officer to use handcuffs, she rose to her feet and agreed to cooperate. We watched as she willingly accompanied the officer to the ambulance and gave consent for paramedics to secure her onto a gurney. The scene nearly broke our hearts, but we were entirely spent and in crisis.

As we followed the ambulance we realized it was providential that the episode happened at our church. Our home and church sat in entirely different counties, and the church held a Cincinnati address. Because of this, Bethany qualified for transport to a major psychiatric trauma center which was located in downtown Cincinnati, instead of a smaller, less progressive psychiatric ward in the county where we lived.

While my husband drove, I made phone contact with a professional colleague who worked in the Psychiatric Emergency Services Department at the hospital. We were in need of moral support. I hoped that through my professional contacts, Bethany's unique situation would be clearly explained to the psychiatrist on duty. Our goal was to have her admitted.

When we arrived at the emergency room entrance, the paramedics were taking Bethany out of the ambulance. She looked vulnerable and frightened as she lay on the gurney. When she noticed us standing nearby, she said she loved us. We assured her that we loved her too. It was painful to see her in such a pitiable situation, and with sadness, we maintained a businesslike posture. We believed if we allowed our emotions to soften our position, she would not feel the seriousness of her condition or her critical need for treatment. Also, we had become so depleted that we had little left to offer her.

While paramedics checked her into the emergency room, we sat in the chaotic waiting area, overwhelmed by the events of the day. After a rather long and anxious period of time, a nurse came out and said we could see her. Although Bethany appeared visibly shaken, she was somehow managing her emotions. The starkness of the room filled with bustling and loud activity, made her appear especially small and alone. But she was cooperating with the hospital staff in every way.

Her dad and I were taken into a room and interviewed by a social worker. We described how we brought Bethany home to live with us after a sixteen-day psychiatric hospitalization and reported that she refused to take her prescribed medication. The heartbreaking story of our long estrangement tumbled out along with an account of our daughter's promising life and her deterioration into a homeless existence. We said we were exhausted from trying to manage her extreme restlessness, and in the night we heard her walking around the house. This patient, professional woman listened while we unloaded our pent up frustration and concerns.

The social worker was sympathetic, recognizing our distress and exhaustion. She encouraged us to go home. She said the assessment process would keep Bethany very busy. She also expected Bethany to be admitted. After speaking with our daughter one more time and telling her we would return the next day, we headed through a series of short corridors toward the hospital exit. As we stepped out into the street, we felt a distinct separation from the permeating chaos of the hospital emergency room and our daughter's troubled life which had overtaken every aspect of our lives. Although we felt guilty leaving her alone, we also felt relieved. We had done all we could but our best efforts had not been enough.

With Bethany in the hospital, our home once again felt like a refuge. But everywhere we looked, little things reminded us of her. As the evening wore on, we waited anxiously to receive a call from the hospital confirming Bethany's admission. After several hours the phone rang and we were finally able to exhale. She was admitted. On the following morning we discovered since she was no longer homeless and since she had been calm and clearly able to express herself, she had come extremely close to being denied admission to the psychiatric ward. If she had been turned down for admission, she would have been released directly back into our care, and our lives would have continued on just as before.

Throughout the short hospitalization we drove downtown every day after work so we could spend time with Bethany. Our limited but concentrated interactions in the hospital setting provided a forum for frank and open discussion. As we reviewed the chain of events leading to her hospital admission, we explained how rundown and hopeless we had become by watching her life deteriorate. In reaffirming our commitment to her, we told her that she was only welcome to return to our home if she agreed to take medication. She shared with us how shocked she had become when realizing that once again she had met the criteria for psychiatric hospitalization. By landing in a mental health unit twice in two months, she was forced to consider the fact that she might actually have something wrong with her.

Prior to this second hospitalization Bethany may have rationalized the deterioration of her life as a result of people interfering with her plans. However, the seriousness of two psychiatric hospital admissions seemed to broaden her perspective. We were deeply thankful for her background in science, because despite her confused mind, she was able to recognize and respect that the diagnostic conclusions of so many medical professionals carried a burden of proof.

On the day of her discharge the three of us sat together with a psychiatrist as he sketched a graph of descending peaks and plateaus on a piece of paper. The stable plateaus represented medication compliance. The lines which plunged downward, away from the plateaus represented discontinuation of treatment and resultant brain deterioration. The doctor explained that every time she stopped taking her medication, even if she resumed taking it later, she would permanently forfeit her former level of functioning and permanently lower her capacity for recovery. Together we understood medication would help settle her mind and allow her to improve her ability to focus her thoughts.

During this meeting the doctor said he was aware of Bethany's academic accomplishments, and being listed as an author of scientific research publications. He offered her hope toward recovery and the possibility of reclaiming her goals. In recognizing her uniqueness and value as an individual, and not treating her like just another psychiatric patient, he offered her a vital and powerful lifeline which she was quick to embrace.

Because Bethany was hospitalized as a result of medication noncompliance, the psychiatrist ordered her Risperdal to be administered in a timed-release injection instead of daily oral doses. The injections would need to be repeated every two weeks. After receiving an injection on the day of discharge, Bethany made a firm commitment to willingly comply with oral medication so she would not have to continue being injected. The enlightening information and encouragement she received from the psychiatrist made sense to her. She gained valuable insight into her illness.

The five days spent in the hospital served to be the major turning point in her life. She understood and accepted the fact that she was being affected by mental illness caused by a chemical imbalance in her brain. She also gained a clear understanding that she could expect medication to effectively settle her mind and allow her to rebuild her life. When she returned to our home she assumed full responsibility for her medication.

Our interactions with her ceased to be confrontational and centered on recovery and future plans. It started to feel like we were all pulling together in the same direction. In gaining a deeper awareness of her mental illness, Bethany began to recognize the enormous toll it had taken on all areas of her life. Yet there was no need to let a diagnosis define her as a person. Despite her journey through personal devastation and homelessness, she was still a unique and gifted individual.

With our encouragement, she finally began to settle into her bedroom. She no longer considered herself a visitor in our home. At the same time, we pledged to stand by her and faithfully work toward our goal of having her reclaim an independent life. The hospitalization had not only provided Bethany with a new perspective, but by having her out of our home for a few days, we had been given an emotional reprieve which enabled us to make a fresh start.

TWENTY-NINE

After a series of frustrations we were finally successful in securing initial psychiatry and counseling appointments for Bethany through a community mental health agency. These appointments would take place just a couple of weeks after her discharge from the hospital. The injection she received while on the psychiatric ward was a special timed-release formula of Risperdal which had a two-week delay. Unfortunately, the full effect of the injection closely coincided with her first appointment with her new psychiatrist. Even though her oral dose had been adjusted and then temporarily discontinued to accommodate the effect of the injection, Bethany appeared sluggish and overly drugged. Because of this we were concerned that the psychiatrist would get an inaccurate first impression of our daughter.

The restless, chaotic energy Bethany experienced during her weeks of medication refusal had swiftly transitioned into an emotionally dull existence. She said she was inwardly suffering from an odd mix of inner restlessness and lethargy which were listed as side effects of her medication. It was like an invisible veil covered her face, separating her from us and the world around her.

When riding in the car, she needed reminders to look at the scenery. At the grocery store she was unable to find specific items without our assistance. Although we took long walks together in the evenings and she still spent time in the library and walking around the community by herself, she spent an increasing amount of time lying on the couch exhausted, watching videos. We noticed her gait had become slower and more awkward and she had a diminished capacity for experiencing joy.

Even though we were relieved to have secured a psychiatry appointment date, in an unbelievably odd way, we felt pulled by a protective parental instinct to avoid interaction with the world of professional psychiatry. Although illogical, it was painful to see her suffer the miserable side effects of her medication. It hurt our hearts. A life of dull exhaustion with inner restlessness was not what we wanted for our daughter. However, having just lived through tortured years of watching her life spin out of control, we were firmly grounded in reality. Through the years we had learned a powerful lesson about her need for treatment. Despite our unspoken feelings, we continued to encourage and support Bethany while she faithfully self-administered every single dose of medication, exactly as prescribed.

During the first appointment, her new psychiatrist immediately recognized her overly drugged state and decreased her medication dosage. He met privately with Bethany, but allowed us time to share our own observations with him and her assigned counselor. The psychiatrist encouraged us to advocate for Bethany's recovery.

Well before the conclusion of the hour-long appointment, the psychiatrist confidently declared Bethany's diagnosis to be schizoaffective disorder, a mental illness having features of both schizophrenia and bipolar disorder.

Up until that definitive moment my husband and I had nurtured just a whisper of secret hope that somehow, her diagnosis would end up being less formal and distinct. It had been illogical but comforting to imagine, that despite two hospital evaluations, she was experiencing just a temporary psychosis which over time in a stable environment would burn itself out and release her. When this experienced older psychiatrist so conclusively stated his diagnosis, we knew the label of mental illness was permanently branded on Bethany's young life. Our reserved hope that the label would somehow be annulled instantly disintegrated and blew away.

The progress of Bethany's recovery unfolded right alongside our established lives in a quiet sort of surrender. Medication allowed her to better recognize and understand how her illness dynamically changed the direction of her life. This understanding illuminated everything she had lost and caused her to grieve. Her life was clearly just a shadow of what it had been in high school and her first years in college. Her father and I empathized with her as we truly recognized her loss.

Photographs of Bethany, taken during this period of time, reflect calmness in her expression. But behind her gentle smile she bravely endured a large measure of suffering. Even though her Risperdal dosage was lowered to reduce the severity of side effects, she still struggled with inner restlessness, fatigue and emotional dullness. And on top of that, the side effect of continual hunger caused her to add nearly ten pounds to her small frame. The increased body weight greatly bothered her and it negatively affected her self-image.

Despite waging a continuous battle against lethargy, Bethany continued to spend time at the public library. And on days when she felt up to it, she still visited me in my office during lunchtime. She balanced these and other activities by sleeping sixteen to eighteen hours each night and by alternating physical activities with time on the couch watching videos. Since her hospitalization, she no longer spent time in the church with the stained glass windows. We encouraged her to meet people her own age and assisted her in finding a few groups to attend. When a generous friend gave her a lovely old violin, she joined our church worship team on a limited basis, and on a few occasions she totally drained her physical reserve to be featured as a soloist.

Despite her symptoms, and her inability to concentrate enough to read a book, we were grateful she was still able to play the violin, the piano, and review foreign language vocabulary even though it was on a very limited basis. In a sense, these abilities became her lifeline. Music was a strong link to her past and enabled her to dream of a brighter future.

Although we included Bethany in our lives and encouraged her to attend activities with many of the people who reached out to her, she was always exhausted and unable to fully experience the joy of living. At times we would notice her gazing into the distance in a type of withdrawal from her surroundings. We did not know if she was just daydreaming or reflecting on specific thoughts.

Unfortunately, Bethany lacked the energy and endurance to work alongside me in my flower garden. Instead, she sat in a chair on our backyard deck and watched me work while I dealt silently with an ever-present sorrow from seeing her so profoundly affected by illness and the side effects of her medication.

When we sat together for any prolonged period of time, I closely observed for untoward physical manifestations from the Risperdal. But I was careful to be discreet, as I did not want her to feel like a patient and view me as her nurse. When sitting still, her legs spontaneously and subtly twitched and her hands never appeared to relax.

Shortly after her hospital discharge she willingly fulfilled the requirements for obtaining Medicaid and Social Security Disability benefits. She was completely aware of medical records we had in our possession from her two hospitalizations which detailed her diagnosis and inability to work, but she chose not to read them. We encouraged her to view disability income as a bridge toward regaining independence, and a funding source for eventually moving into her own apartment.

In early summer 2007 Bethany's psychiatrist transitioned her to a newer but similar medication called Invega. Although she continued to experience side effects similar to Risperdal, they were less intense and disabling. This change allowed her to draw a small amount of pleasure out of life, but did not entirely eliminate the chemical "veil" that blunted personality. She remained limited in her ability to engage in bright and dynamic conversation with other people, and we rarely heard her laugh. Also, after being on the new medication for only three weeks, she gained an additional ten pounds of body weight. In a broad sense, things were better, but she was still far from realizing true recovery because the Invega did not effectively calm her mind.

We were quick to learn that through the community mental health agency, Bethany had very limited access to her psychiatrist. If her suffering intensified and she needed her medication dosage adjusted, it was very challenging to connect directly with the doctor. After the initial meetings with her psychiatrist, she was left to wait four weeks between appointments. This was especially distressing because in our opinion she was still far from landing on a plateau of wellness and stability.

In late summer, members of our extended family gathered for a reunion near a lake in Wisconsin. Bethany reconnected with people whom she had not seen for many years. Although she spoke with many of them by phone around the time of her first hospitalization, it was wonderful to see them embrace in person.

It was especially touching to watch the interaction between Bethany and her brother. He had flown in from out of state, and it was their first reunion after a separation of five years. He treated her with gentleness and compassion.

Although it warmed our hearts to see her participate in water sports with her brother and cousins, it was difficult to watch her struggle against her restless mind and the side effects of her medication. Throughout our time in Wisconsin it saddened us to witness her constrained attempts to enjoy her life.

As weeks passed, Invega began to improve Bethany's ability to focus her thoughts, enabling her to begin reading light works of fiction. It seemed as though the medication empowered her to better separate herself from her symptoms, but side effects from the drug continued to hold her back from returning to a normal life. Despite all of this, she expressed a strong desire to return to college.

She and her dad toured the main campus of the University of Cincinnati and she loved it. We encouraged her to submit an application. As we looked toward the future we realized her recovery would encompass every area of her life and most likely progress one small step at a time. There was no way to know how far she could go in reclaiming her academic dreams. Unfortunately, even though she was able to read, she continued to experience an impaired ability to deeply concentrate which thwarted her ability to study.

Shortly after her visit to the campus, Bethany surprised us by contacting a medical professor at the university who was engaged in a specific type of research. His field of study related to research projects she had worked on in the past. Despite her daily battle against lethargy, she secured an appointment date with the professor and was compelled to study his publications. We watched as she pushed herself, exhausting every last bit of physical and mental energy. The meeting went well and the professor seemed impressed with her knowledge, but over time, lethargy and her illness prevented her from retaining this contact. She was unable to meet with him a second time, forfeiting her chance to pursue an opportunity in scientific research. The physical limitation of fatigue along with impaired concentration blocked her path at every turn.

One afternoon in late August 2007, Bethany called me while I was at work. With tentative words, she admitted to hearing voices in her mind. This statement caught me off guard because up to this point she had firmly denied ever experiencing this symptom. It was a strange and terrible thing to hear from my own daughter and my initial reaction was to recoil in unbelief. But she was sincere, risking total honesty with an earnest desire to recover from her illness. The new revelation better explained her continuing inability to focus her thoughts. I left work, and found her sitting calmly in a lawn chair on our back deck. Although I found the symptom distressing, it was nothing new to her and she seemed surprised that I felt an urgent need to leave work early.

As we talked together, she explained how she had been hearing voices in her mind for a long time, and said it was the main reason she could not concentrate. She believed the time had finally come to let us know.

Throughout her first hospitalization, the psychiatrist had been certain Bethany was hearing voices. This auditory hallucination is a manifestation of a chemical imbalance in the brain. The voices are actually the person's own thoughts, similar to scolding yourself in your mind or having a song persistently stuck in your head. The sustained presence of this hallucination powerfully illustrated her severe illness and the ineffectiveness of her medication. As Bethany agreed to openly share this information with her psychiatrist, we became hopeful that a more effective medication might be found which would enable her to live a healthy and normal life.

THIRTY

Just as summer was turning into fall Bethany let us know that one morning, out of sheer frustration, she hit herself. She had been lying in bed and unable to get up because the voices in her mind were utterly intolerable. As she lay there inwardly suffering, through an open window she overheard the joyful laughter of neighborhood children waiting to board a school bus in front of our house. The sweet sounds overwhelmed her emotions as she mourned the loss of her own childhood and the simple human dignity of having a meaningful reason to get out of bed. If she were ever to truly live again, she would need to regain a clear mind and an increased measure of physical energy.

Along with being more open with her psychiatrist, Bethany agreed to an idea we had about seeking a case manager through a local mental health service provider. We intended to exhaust every available resource in order to promote a steady and full recovery. We questioned whether an hourly or part-time job could be found which could offer a sort of halfway step, or a bridge between doing nothing and returning to school. It was around this time that Bethany received a letter of acceptance from the University of Cincinnati. Unfortunately she was not well enough to enroll in even one class.

A case manager was assigned to meet with her once a month. But it did not take long to realize that typical mental health case management services would not even begin to meet her needs. Because Bethany was able to converse with the case manager like a professional colleague, the manager was unable to truly understand the unique nature of her illness and situation, along with the vision she still held for her future.

Bethany's father assisted her in exploring opportunities for employment in our community but during the quest to help her find purpose, it became clear that there would be no halfway point. Medication ineffectiveness and side effects held her back from working even a simple hourly job. If medication could not be found to effectively treat her, we realized she would be left to endure a sort of half-life, trapped in the disabling realm of mental illness.

In early fall, the psychiatrist prescribed an additional medication called Abilify. When Bethany took her first dose, the blanket of lethargy, and the veil that shrouded her personality began to dissipate and she came alive. It was an amazing and joyful turn of events, like clouds parting to reveal the sun. The daughter we once knew was returning to us. After months of misery, we rejoiced with her as it looked as though an effective drug had finally been found. But joy was abruptly snuffed out. Abilify, prescribed at a low dosage, caused Bethany to experience the rare hallucination of physical pain, so the drug was promptly discontinued. As the medication was withdrawn, we helplessly watched as she retreated back into her isolating illness. It took faith and daily fortitude to push against a strong current of discouragement and despair that always seemed ready to engulf us.

Somehow Bethany managed to live just above the level of hopelessness. But on a day-to-day basis, a dark cloud seemed to hang heavily over our entire house. We were grateful when our friends reached out to her in many ways with a steady stream of invitations, and a grandmother in our church lovingly befriended her. But unfortunately, severe lethargy forced her to decline many of the invitations.

Although hope remained alive, all three of us lived in a house of suffering. In my heart, I struggled against deep sorrow and guilt. Sorrow for the productive life Bethany had lost, and guilt about having a healthy mind and the ability to function well in my own career. Because my emotions were raw, I protected myself by limiting the amount of information I was willing to share with people outside our family. I refrained from disclosing specific medical details to all but a few of my most trusted professional colleagues. Their expertise and insight was a foundational element in our survival as a family. In my daily work I developed a deeper passion for those on my caseload with mental illness. But the ironic and cruel twist to it all was that my expanding knowledge and advocacy in the field of mental health seemed to benefit my patients more than my own daughter.

Each day the distinct color of chronic sorrow was tightly woven into the fabric of our lives. At times my mind rebelled and I imagined different ways I could escape the pain of watching my daughter struggle against her severe illness and the oppressive influence it exerted upon each one of us. The support of family and friends was crucial, but it was God's faithfulness that truly sustained us.

In fall 2007, Bethany's medication was changed because Invega was not effectively treating her symptoms. It was replaced with a medication called Geodon. Prior to starting Geodon, Abilify had been reintroduced at Bethany's request, even though she knew there was a possibility of again experiencing the hallucination of physical pain. She weighed the sensation of intense discomfort in her back against mental anguish, and chose to risk physical pain for a chance at gaining a quieter mind. It was interesting that for Bethany, when Abilify was prescribed the second time at a higher dosage, it did not produce the painful hallucinations. But as she continued to take the drug, it produced far less benefit than she had experienced during the initial drug trial.

As the Geodon was added to the Abilify and the dosage was steadily increased, it began to clear her mind. But the effectiveness of Geodon seemed to peak and then rapidly diminish with each passing week. One outstanding benefit from this drug combination was a decrease in appetite and a loss of a full ten pounds.

THIRTY-ONE

In fall 2007, Bethany's quality of life continued to slowly spiral downward as she struggled against differing levels of fatigue and mental torment.

Her auditory hallucinations seemed to intensify every time she tried to concentrate on anything complex or especially meaningful to her. Although the combination of Abilify and Geodon seemed to have fewer side effects than Invega, this benefit was nullified by the inability of the drugs to sufficiently treat her symptoms. We helplessly watched as she slowly and quietly withdrew from her environment and away from us. She resigned herself to spending many hours each day lying on the couch and watching videos.

Things were not going well, and we found it remarkable to look back and recall all the events that had transpired since receiving the call from the police, just six months earlier. We were frustrated and angry. Our daughter had recognized and accepted her psychiatric diagnosis, she had willingly moved into our home, she was connected to mental health services, and she was fully compliant with every aspect of treatment. As a patient, she was knowledgeable, polite, and courteous. Yet despite it all, the mental torment she endured on a daily basis, in a way, seemed to be more pitiful than the homeless existence she had endured while being unaware of her mental illness. When we had received the call, in an odd way she had seemed happy living her desolate life, and was more capable of vibrantly interacting with other people. It was easy to see how the medicated and tortured life she was living did not in the least bit resemble true recovery. Even though medication had enabled her to gain enough insight to recognize her illness, she was extremely miserable.

On November 15, 2007, Bethany asked to be taken to an emergency room because she was unable to connect with her psychiatrist and her symptoms were more than she could bear. Her dad took her to the University Hospital in Cincinnati, as we believed this to be her best option. Together, she and her dad waited several hours in the uncomfortable and chaotic emergency department so she could be evaluated. The long wait resulted in only a minor dosage change which unfortunately provided her with very minimal relief.

The following week, she was able to secure an extra appointment with her psychiatrist and her medication dosages were once again readjusted. Shortly following this appointment, we took a trip out of state to join family for the Thanksgiving holiday. Despite the dosage adjustment, after about an hour into the long car ride, Bethany told us her symptoms were intensifying. She tried to make contact with her psychiatrist by phone through a social worker at the community health agency but was told that her situation did not sound significant enough to disturb the psychiatrist during his holiday weekend.

Right after returning from our Thanksgiving trip, On December 1, 2007, once again Bethany asked to be taken to the psychiatric emergency room. At this point she was still prescribed the ineffective combination of Abilify and Geodon.

Each time Bethany asked us to drive her downtown to the psychiatric emergency room, I knew it was the result of a carefully weighed decision. In each situation, she had to ask herself if the intensity of the mental pain was worth the risk of potentially waiting four or five hours in a noisy, overcrowded room just to be seen by a psychiatrist. When she made the decision to go, I knew her symptoms were more than she could bear. During this December 1 emergency room visit, the psychiatrist altered her dosages only slightly, and she was sent home to resume her pitiful life.

A few days after the emergency room visit, Bethany met with her community psychiatrist for her monthly appointment. At the conclusion of the meeting, the psychiatrist handed us a piece of notepaper. The paper contained the names of two prominent research psychiatrists associated with the University of Cincinnati. The psychiatrist instructed Bethany and me to pursue one of those physicians for her continuing psychiatric care because the complexity and severity of her illness required a higher degree of expertise than the community mental health agency was able to offer. The discharge was unexpected, fraying the most important professional contact Bethany had, a psychiatrist that had just begun to really know her. Left with a feeling of abandonment, we were dismissed to pursue the research psychiatrists on our own.

Bethany quietly endured as her symptoms intensified. Even though she had been seen by the community psychiatrist only five days prior, she once again felt the need to be taken to the emergency room.

December 6 marked her third visit to the psychiatric emergency department. Somehow she found enough strength to endure hours of waiting to see a psychiatrist, but unfortunately, once again she found little relief from her symptoms. While the discharge from the community psychiatrist and the recommendation to see a research physician offered a warped ray of hope, at the same time we were left feeling insecure and alienated and it was painful watching her endure her illness.

Things were obviously going very badly. But even though Bethany suffered, she maintained a gentle and sweet demeanor. Through it all she never lost sight of her goal to recover, and she remained committed to treatment. This period of time was a very dark chapter in our lives. We could not imagine that things could get much worse, and Bethany's tortuous journey toward recovery seemed like it would never end.

The day after receiving the names of the Cincinnati research psychiatrists, I looked them up on the Internet and found contact information. When I phoned the office of the first physician, I was connected to a professional assistant. She patiently listened while I passionately summarized Bethany's psychiatric history, placing a heavy emphasis on the uniqueness of her case. With kindness, the assistant explained that the research physician did not directly schedule appointments with patients. Feeling disappointed and nervous, I then dialed the number to the second psychiatrist. I repeated my story to a second assistant, and was again told that the doctor did not directly schedule appointments with patients.

The assistant must have sensed panic and urgency in my voice and asked me for Bethany's contact information. She made an offer to refer Bethany's case to the director of a city mental health clinic and fill him in on the nature and severity of Bethany's situation. The assistant explained that the director of the clinic would personally choose a psychiatrist for Bethany. She said we would be contacted by the clinic shortly after the referral was made. Upon hearing this, a feeling of overwhelming relief washed over me. I realized weeks of red tape and delays had just been swept away in my pursuit to find a highly qualified psychiatrist connected to a mental health agency that was willing to accept Medicaid. By taking the time to listen long enough to recognize the serious nature of our situation and by having enough compassion to go the extra mile, this professional mercifully touched our lives. In a rush of pent-up emotion I expressed my heartfelt thanks.

Doubt and fear began to emerge when a week passed without a call from the city clinic. However we realized a great favor had been done for us in securing a referral and we did not want to exert unwelcomed pressure on the clinic employees. It was understandable that it would take time for people to act, so we allowed several more days to pass before calling to inquire about an appointment date. When I finally called, I was transferred to a "gatekeeper" for the clinic. When I explained our situation I was curtly told to be patient, and someone would contact us. I immediately backed off as I did not want to further aggravate the person who seemed to control the appointments.

We waited through another week and still did not receive a call. At this point we believed there was no choice but to risk another phone call. The woman I was transferred to explained that psychiatrists were less available during the Christmas season, and she instructed me to call after the first of the year.

In early January I made a third call and was connected to a different "gatekeeper." I was grateful when she gave me a date for an intake appointment with a psychiatrist, but disappointed that it was not scheduled until late February. This meant that Bethany would have to somehow survive without a psychiatric appointment for two more months.

On January 11, 2008, Bethany again returned to the psychiatric emergency department, and again found little relief. It was actually her fifth emergency room visit, as during her fourth trip downtown she chose to leave without being seen by a psychiatrist because she could not tolerate the interminable wait. When she heard the expected waiting time was in excess of six hours, she realized it was beyond her level of endurance.

With extreme lethargy, Bethany dragged herself through each day, held captive by the turmoil in her mind. She seemed to survive by spending an increasing amount of time lying on the couch watching mindless videos, but due to an impaired ability to concentrate, she did not seem to actually focus on them. They served only as a means to help pass the time because she was waiting. Waiting for the appointment with her new psychiatrist and waiting to recover her life. And through it all, a feeling of extreme heaviness continued to permeate our home.

On January 25, 2008 Bethany again returned to the psychiatric emergency department. Her dad was the one who took her each time, and stayed with her while she waited. After several hours passed, she was finally seen by a nurse practitioner. The nurse explained to Bethany that emergency room physicians preferred not to make major changes in medication due to their inability to provide follow-up care. The nurse went on to inform her that she should not be using the emergency room as a primary psychiatrist. When Bethany replied that she did not have an appointment until late February, the nurse practitioner encouraged her to wait patiently for that appointment.

THIRTY-TWO

With frustration, we watched as Bethany quietly retreated into her illness. Around 8 PM on February 4, 2008, she took her medicine and went to bed. My husband and I turned in around ten thirty. About an hour later we were jolted awake by a pitiful and torturous cry. It was the outflow of severe mental anguish and an involuntary plea for help which could not be ignored. I went into her room and asked her if she felt strong enough to sit with me in the hospital emergency room. When she said she was willing to try, we hastily dressed and began our journey downtown.

It was after midnight when we arrived at the hospital, and nearly 1 AM when we were instructed to sit in the psychiatric waiting area. The room was very cold, so we decided to keep our coats and mittens on. We were dreadfully aware that our waiting time would be determined by the number of people checked in before us and also by the number of ambulances which were sure to arrive, carrying people in need of immediate attention.

It was Friday night, and one of the emergency room's busiest times. Bethany was in crisis and I had just lived through an exceptionally long and busy workday. We were both exhausted. Because it was the middle of the night, we found the bright and glaring fluorescent lights to be especially annoying, and the cold and rigid plastic chairs prohibited any sort of comfortable posture.

It was impossible not to notice, on the other side of the room, an apparently homeless man slept soundly, sprawled across the only two chairs not separated by an angular armrest. Initially there were about ten of us in the waiting room, but shortly after our arrival a few of them were called back into the treatment rooms. This gave us hope. But as time went by, sounds of yelling and screaming began to drift out from behind one of the side doors, and we got the impression that the place was extremely busy. When I asked the receptionist about an estimated waiting time, she told me there was no way to predict how long it would take to see a psychiatrist.

Bethany did her best to curl up in one of the chairs as she closed her eyes against the bright light. The black and white wall clock became a focal point for me. The television was loud and controlled by a young man who also appeared to be waiting to see a psychiatrist. He laughed loudly while watching back-to-back episodes of crude situational comedies with accompanying laugh tracks. As Bethany readjusted herself in her chair, I attempted to put on a hopeful face and encouraged her to hang on.

Sitting there with nothing to do but wait, I tried to imagine what the people looked like who were yelling and screaming behind the treatment room door. Along with the screaming and yelling, we were also privy to a mix of angry outbursts, laughter, and periods of silence. I wondered about the people sitting around us, as unkempt clothing and odd mannerisms revealed clues about their lives. The waiting area of a psychiatric emergency room is without doubt a miserable and disturbing place.

Around 3 AM I again asked the receptionist for a general estimate on when we would be called back into the treatment room. She told me it could be another three hours, and possibly more than four, depending on the change of shift. She qualified that her estimate could not be guaranteed. Bethany and I were trapped in a tough situation. A few times she offered to just go home so we could go to bed, but that no longer seemed to be a realistic option.

Periodically I encouraged her to keep soldiering on, as I could see how difficult it was for her to manage her symptoms in the over-stimulating environment. Both of us greatly yearned to be in our own beds. The chair I was sitting in was positioned directly across from the waiting room receptionist who sat just behind a clear glass window. The size of the window allowed a direct view into the area where patient records appeared to be kept, and where professional staff appeared to read those records and write their case notes. I noticed how two women in white coats casually chatted together behind a desk. They seemed to be just passing through a regular night at work. But for us, the night was far from regular. The waiting room of the psychiatric emergency department was not the place we wanted to be. We had come because it was our only option, and in our crisis, we had nowhere else to turn. By being alienated from a primary psychiatrist in the community, Bethany had become practically faceless.

Time slowly crept by, and around 5 AM Bethany's name was finally called. She got up and walked through the treatment room door to be assessed by a social worker. After about fifteen minutes she was released back into the waiting room. The social worker asked if she could speak privately with me and Bethany gave her consent. I followed the woman into a screening room and told my version of Bethany's history and current situation. The woman attentively listened while I spoke and then told me she had taken the time to carefully read Bethany's medical records. She stated that in her opinion, Bethany needed to be hospitalized.

Her statement caught me completely off guard as I had been mentally preparing myself to aggressively plead Bethany's case. When she immediately recognized the severity of Bethany's condition, I struggled to contain my emotions and expressed deep wholehearted thanks for her professional skill, her understanding, and her compassion.

When I returned to the waiting room to explain to Bethany what had transpired, my whole body began to shiver with cold. I realized it was not only a reaction to the chilly waiting room and lack of sleep, but also a total surrender into the emotional duress we endured for so many long hours just to gain access to emergency psychiatric care.

Bethany was ushered back into the treatment room area, and in a state of weary submission she allowed herself to be assisted onto a hospital gurney. The social worker told me that Bethany would be evaluated by a psychiatrist as soon as one was available and reiterated that she would strongly advocate for hospital admission. About an hour later I left the hospital alone, emotionally and physically spent. I was deeply grateful for the compassionate social worker who took the time to look beyond appointment dates and medication changes to truly see the depth of Bethany's intense suffering.

From the moment we received the call from the police in March 2007, our lives were forcefully thrust into the world of mental illness. With our daughter's life at stake, we had embarked upon an arduous journey. Life had become joyless and oppressive. Repeated attempts to help Bethany restore her life seemed always to result in disappointment. We had followed the rules and acted on the advice of so many mental health professionals, but despite our efforts and Bethany's willing compliance with treatment, she had somehow defaulted into a wasteland of misery.

Our marriage had taken a beating. Even though my husband and I remained strongly committed to one another, we felt ragged and empty from our year-long search to find healing for our daughter and from helplessly watching her suffer. It was an enormous relief to have Bethany hospitalized where we hoped she would be reevaluated and offered a fresh start.

THIRTY-THREE

My husband and I felt deeply saddened because we knew how much Bethany detested being confined in a psychiatric ward. Together and individually we dealt with guilt for having failed her. Because she was so ill, it was difficult to think about her having to endure varying degrees of chaotic noise from other patients on the unit, and a room with very little privacy.

As soon as we arrived home from our jobs each day, we headed downtown to spend time with Bethany. Although it was plain to see that she continued to suffer, she spoke hopefully about having been interviewed by several different mental health professionals. A few of the doctors seemed to take special interest in the profound details of her story.

When the three of us met together with one of her psychiatrists we were grateful to learn that a comprehensive battery of medical tests had been ordered for her. We were impressed by the doctor's keen interest in attempting to isolate a medical reason which could account for the intractable and persistent nature of Bethany's symptoms.

As a psychiatric patient, Bethany possessed an unusual self-awareness and insight. She had the ability to accurately and intelligently recall a sequence of exact dates and times associated with the progression of her illness. She was polite, friendly, and appreciated opportunities to converse with medical professionals. Her background in science empowered her to accurately describe what it was like to experience the manifestations of psychosis, and live with specific side effects from medication. Her case quickly attracted special attention because she offered medical professionals a clear window through which they could view the inner workings of severe mental illness.

During this hospitalization we allowed ourselves to guardedly hope for a new effective treatment and possibly even a cure. Obsessive compulsive personality disorder with psychosis was the new diagnosis because one of the psychiatrists recognized Bethany's history of compulsive violin practice in high school and her exceptionally strong drive to excel in academics. It looked as though everything was being questioned and reevaluated.

Because none of the standard psychiatric medications were managing Bethany's symptoms, the psychiatrist decided to give her a short trial of Depakote which is an anticonvulsant drug. This helped to rule out the question of whether or not her symptoms could be related to an obscure seizure disorder. A determination was quickly made that her hallucinations were not seizure related. There was also question whether the antimalarial drug Malarone was a factor in causing her psychosis, because Bethany had taken this drug while in Africa. As it turned out, there was no way to know for certain if the medication had in any way influenced her mental health.

At the conclusion of one of the physician assessments, Bethany gave legal consent which would allow her case to be presented during a Psychiatric Grand Rounds meeting at the University Hospital in Cincinnati, where psychiatrists and mental health professionals gathered to discuss interesting and complex cases. This presentation would occur later in the spring.

Right before her discharge, Bethany was given a short trial of the drugs Zyprexa and Lexapro. When Zyprexa failed to quiet the voices in her mind, the hospital psychiatrist restarted Invega as her primary medication. She had been weaned off Invega during the previous fall with the hope that her symptoms would improve on a combination of two other medications, Geodon and Abilify. Although her symptoms had not improved, the drug combination caused fewer side effects, which allowed her personality to reemerge from underneath a heavy blanket of sedation. In a sense, she had come back to us. But in being less sedated, the symptoms of her mental illness affected her more severely, and those symptoms also took her away from us. She was left with a cruel choice of being heavily sedated or intensely suffering. Within hours of restarting Invega in the hospital, we watched as she reassumed an emotionally blunted and drugged appearance. It was deeply distressing to witness, but we knew the transformation was the cruel tradeoff for gaining a small measure of relief from the voices in her mind.

The hospitalization had lasted nine days. Even though the change in diagnosis brought a measure of hope, it seemed as though little improvement had been made in Bethany's quality of life beyond being recognized and better understood. We looked forward to the initial appointment with her new primary psychiatrist, which was scheduled for the week after her hospital discharge.

THIRTY-FOUR

At the end of February 2008, both her father and I accompanied Bethany to an appointment with her new psychiatrist. We were grateful that due to her recent hospitalization, the new doctor would have plenty of medical records to look through which we hoped would provide new insight into her complex case.

Bethany's personality was markedly blunted on the day of her first appointment. After introductions, the psychiatrist was very direct in explaining to us that he preferred to treat patients using the concept of monotherapy, which is the prescribing of only one drug at a time. He said he would increase Bethany's dosage of Invega to a fairly high, therapeutic level. This was in contrast to using a combination of multiple drugs at lower, sub-therapeutic levels.

Up to this point, with the exception of Abilify, it appeared that Bethany only tolerated medication prescribed at lower dosages. It seemed that when dosages increased, the drugs merely contributed to her suffering. Heavy side effects caused her an added dimension of misery. At the conclusion of that first appointment, the psychiatrist decisively changed the diagnosis back to schizoaffective disorder. Invega was the only drug prescribed to Bethany and the dosage would increase in an incremental manner.

During her second psychiatry appointment, Bethany reported only marginal improvement with the voices in her mind, and she appeared disengaged and lethargic. Also, due to an increased appetite she had rapidly regained ten pounds.

At home, she spent most of her time sleeping or lying on the couch, occasionally drawing upon her limited store of energy to push herself into activities that did not require a lot of physical energy. Her personality was dull and dispirited. It was heartbreaking to watch her silently withdraw from the joy of life.

Due to the persistent nature of Bethany's symptoms, the psychiatrist eventually prescribed the drug Zyprexa in addition to Invega. Unfortunately the combination of these drugs at higher therapeutic levels did not quiet her mind. We felt as if we had lost our daughter to her illness and the heavy side effects produced by the drugs. At this point, a mental health professional at the clinic urged us to enroll Bethany in a mental health day program which he claimed would facilitate her recovery. It would provide a place for her to go each day where she could join a therapy group and socialize with other mentally ill patients.

Everything seemed wrong. We knew that the voices in Bethany's mind were a manifestation of a chemical imbalance in her brain. Counseling and therapy groups would not correct the imbalance. We were deeply disillusioned by the options the world of psychiatry was offering our daughter. It felt like we had ended our journey by crashing into a cement barrier. It was obvious that unless a medication could effectively treat the chemical imbalance in her brain, the door to any sort of meaningful future would remain closed to her. And she still wanted desperately to have her life back.

The three of us spent a lot of time discussing what we should to do next. It was confusing because she was so limited by her symptoms and the side effects of the medication, and we felt like there was nowhere to turn.

After considering her lethargy and the aversion we all had to a day program, Bethany decided to spend her days at home. Though her energy was limited, she could play uncomplicated music on her violin and engage in simple activities. We wanted her to find joy wherever she could in her oppressive life. We were grateful for friends and family who reached out to her at this time. Although she continued to silently suffer, she tried to find contentment in little things.

A few months later, toward the end of spring 2008, a University Hospital psychiatrist invited Bethany to attend the Grand Rounds meeting where her case was scheduled to be presented. She willingly submitted to being interviewed in front of a whole room of medical professionals. Because of her scientific background, she understood the importance of sharing her unique story in the professional realm.

During the presentation, Bethany described the details of her decline into mental illness with remarkable insight. With intelligence and precision she explained what it felt like to experience the hallucination of voices and the ways that specific psychiatric drugs affected her.

As a result of the Grand Rounds experience, an amazing thing happened. One of the prominent research psychiatrists Bethany had been so loosely referred to back in December 2007, who we had unsuccessfully pursued, offered to personally assume the management of her psychiatric care. Not only did the physician recognize the depth of her suffering, but also her potential for a full recovery. He committed himself to keeping her from falling into the cracks of the imperfect mental healthcare system.

THIRTY-FIVE

After nearly nine long years of being acutely affected by mental illness, the direction of Bethany's life took a dramatic turn toward genuine healing and recovery. Under her new psychiatrist's care, Bethany was slowly transitioned to an older, psychiatric medication called Clozaril while everything else was being discontinued.

Clozaril is usually reserved for people with "treatment resistant" symptoms, because the side effect profile includes the risk of a sudden and possibly severe reduction of white blood cells. People who take Clozaril are mandated to submit to weekly blood testing for the first several months of treatment. Once the psychiatrist determines that the drug is being safely tolerated, blood testing is usually decreased to every two weeks until it finally levels out at once monthly. Despite Bethany's strong aversion to needles, she eagerly agreed to the drug trial and all the required blood testing.

Up until this point, no drug had provided Bethany with true symptom relief. Despite enduring extreme fatigue and other miserable side effects, she had not even come close to a recovery from her illness. There had been so many trials of so many drugs attached to so many promises, and each time her hopes had been dashed.

As weeks went by, the dosage of Clozaril was gradually increased until it reached a therapeutic range. There was no sense of instant healing, but over time Bethany began to perceive a gentle quieting of her mind. The thick cloud of oppressive illness slowly began to release her. With each passing month we watched as step by step she walked further away from the center of the cloud of mental illness.

Bethany's increased ability to concentrate freed her to read all sorts of books, play her violin more extensively, and broaden her study of foreign languages. Along with her steady recovery, deep-seated doubt began to loosen its tight grip on all of our lives.

As more months passed, recovery seemed to build upon recovery and sustained levels of improvement validated her treatment.

Her zest for life and appreciation for humor slowly returned. Laughter began to drift into our lives. The healthy daughter we had once known was gradually restored to us. She eventually emerged as a person with a quiet and healthy mind. Everyone who knew her witnessed a slow but incredible transformation process.

Although Clozaril is known for being a drug which causes significant weight gain, Bethany did not experience this side effect. As her appetite decreased she was able to gradually lose the weight she had gained from several of the previously prescribed medications. However, fatigue continued to physically drag her down.

As I turn the pages of our family album and view photographs from summer 2008 through late spring 2009, I see the subtle signs of Bethany's recovery. The signs are visible not only in her physical appearance but in her spirit which radiates through her smile and in the increasingly confident way she presents herself through the series of photographs. Against all odds, she triumphed over severe mental illness, and was set free to once again experience the essence of health and the vibrancy of life.

As I continue turning the pages of our family album, once again I see her dressed in concert black, proudly holding her violin. This photograph dates to April 2009. It is the night before Easter and her face beams with pride. Shortly after I took this picture, her father and I watched with overwhelming joy as she took her seat in a professional orchestra to perform the musical score of Handel's *Messiah*. The colorful thread of our daughter's recovery has brightly fortified the fabric of our lives.

As months continued to pass and seasons changed, Bethany explored and rediscovered areas of her life which had been closed to her for many years. It was like watching her walk down a long hallway and open door after door along the way, each door representing a reclaimed area of special interest. She became more sociable and active in conversations as her awareness of current events sharpened. As her suffering lessened, she was able to invest more of her energy into friendships with family and special people. The progression of her recovery was slow moving but steady because she faithfully took her medication day after day and never skipped a dose. She knew that her healthy life depended upon it.

In spring 2009 Bethany received a renewal of her acceptance into the University of Cincinnati. She had progressed to the point of having just enough confidence to enroll in one class for the following fall. She wanted to test her ability to focus and study, and test the limits of her physical endurance. Although Clozaril effectively eliminated her symptoms, she continued to battle against the side effect of fatigue. This required her to spend at least twelve hours in bed each day. Since our home was an inconvenient distance from the university, and since she had reached and maintained a level of true recovery, we knew it was time to take the next step.

Throughout Bethany's illness all three of us had become emotionally attached to one another by living in the same house. After what we had all endured prior to her return to Ohio, it was difficult to think about having her move out of our home. But we knew that in order for her to find *complete* restoration, she would have to establish an independent life in a home of her own.

In April 2009, we began to discuss the topic of finding Bethany an apartment near the university. This whole concept rubbed against the grain of all of our lives as it threatened to deeply disturb our very secure comfort levels. We no longer woke in the middle of the night wondering where our daughter was, and Bethany had settled comfortably into our home. But we knew she could not completely recover while being held back by barriers constructed out of our own fear and doubt. No matter how uncomfortable each of us felt about having her leave our home, the fact remained that she was an adult and needed to embrace her own healthy independent life.

During her recovery, Bethany gained an increased awareness of how dangerous her life had become while deeply affected by mental illness. The unclouded view of her risky travel and homeless lifestyle truly frightened her. We spent hours discussing her return to independence, as opposed to remaining in the security of our home. Overcoming her own doubt and fear, in May 2009, she confidently signed a lease on an apartment located just a few blocks from the downtown campus. Together we spent the summer of 2009 collecting the bits and pieces required to furnish an apartment. These preparations helped us to process our emotions. Even though we would live close enough to see each other often, we were all preparing to "let go."

THIRTY-SIX

Self-confidence is built one step at a time, and on September 1, 2009 Bethany took a giant step by moving into her own apartment. A few weeks later she began attending a genetics class. Her return to an academic environment opened up an entire world of new possibilities.

Recovery continued to build upon recovery and she kept striding forward. Each day she studied hard, often asking questions after class, and over time she sought friendships with other students. All this was accomplished while continuing to battle against the heavy side effects of lethargy and fatigue, and the need to sleep at least twelve hours each night. Her efforts paid off when she earned an "A" in the class. Receiving a high grade bolstered enough confidence to sign up for two more classes the following semester in January 2010. Each new accomplishment propelled her forward as she learned just how far she could push herself each day and each semester.

Nothing came easily and nothing happened quickly. There was no simple remedy or magic pill to instantly turn her life around. Instead, there was a gradual transition from deep suffering to recovery just like dawn begins with a whisper of light and then slowly spreads into the brightness of day. Bethany fought for herself every step of the way, improving one day at a time over months and years. Despite our striving, the opportunity for recovery was made possible because a few exceptional mental health professionals cared enough to look past the mask of mental illness to see the valuable person underneath.

On December 10, 2011, Bethany was awarded a Bachelor's Degree in Molecular Biology from the University of Cincinnati. During her graduation ceremony she was one of the first graduates to enter the auditorium. She was dressed in a special red cap and gown which set her apart as a Student Marshall of her class. This was an honor bestowed upon only a few select graduates. There is no way to describe the overwhelming emotion as her dad, brother, and I stood together watching her walk across the stage to receive her diploma. It was impossible to project that after such a tumultuous and dangerous journey through mental illness, she could ever arrive at such a place as this.

Throughout the dark years of Bethany's story, we never could have imagined the future would hold such a day. There had been simply too much suffering, too much pain, and too much illness. Bethany's life had every reason to find a tragic end, but it did not.

I once heard it said that "By giving into despair, we proclaim to know the future." In contrast, by not giving in to despair, hope remains alive. None of us can ever know exactly what lies ahead, but we can all cling to hope. Because of our journey, we have learned without a shadow of a doubt that God is the keeper of our lives. Whatever awaits us in the future, I know that God will faithfully see us through, because I have seen his hand redeem a life.

Acknowledgements

This book exists because our family has survived an unspeakable trial, and against insurmountable odds, we are once again whole. As you may have suspected while turning the pages of my story, I am a Christian and draw my strength from Jesus Christ. With excitement, I look forward to what the future will hold.

My husband David has the wonderful gift of always viewing things from a positive perspective. His encouragement has been vital to me during very dark times. His devotion and love is steadfast and true. Not only is he my husband of over thirty-five years, but also my dearest friend.

I owe a debt of gratitude to Dr. Henry A. Nasrallah, the gifted and compassionate psychiatrist who looked through the heavy mask of mental illness to find a young woman of promise. I will always be thankful that by providence, our paths crossed at just the right time.

I treasure my daughter Bethany and admire her willingness to openly share her story in the writing of her own book, *Mind Estranged*. She encouraged me to compose this companion book in order to present a broader perspective of her journey. May her life be filled with purpose and joy.

I am deeply grateful for family and friends who loved me through my journey and encouraged me in the writing of this book, and for members of my church who love me like family.

Special thanks to Editor Gretchen Dietz for her skillful contributions to my manuscript and to Alex Friedman, for completing the editing and formatting process required to transform my manuscript into book form. I would also like to express my thanks to Ryan Martin for artistic cover design, and Theresa Ware for photography.

About the Author

Karen S. Yeiser is a registered nurse, and the mother of two adult children. During the span of her nursing career she devoted twenty-two years to the care of adults with developmental disabilities. While living through the crisis in her daughter's life, she gained a deeper understanding of mental illness. She hopes to enlighten people about the devastating effects untreated mental illness can exert on individuals and family members, and stimulate new interest toward the possibility of recovery. She lives in Ohio with her husband, David.

Flight from Reason is her first book.

Further Reading

Mind Estranged:
My Journey from Schizophrenia and Homelessness to Recovery
A memoir by Bethany Yeiser

Mind Estranged is the companion book to *Flight from Reason: A Mother's Story of Schizophrenia, Recovery and Hope*

Mind Estranged is Bethany's story, written from her perspective, which takes the reader into the bizarre and isolating symptoms of emerging schizophrenia. Confused, and unaware of her mental illness, she dropped out of college, traveled to three continents, and eventually became homeless on the streets of a West Coast city.

Bethany draws you into her deteriorating mind and into the devastation of being homeless as she vividly describes her schizophrenic world of delusions and hallucinations. Eventually, and against all odds, she made a complete recovery and graduated from college.

Mind Estranged parallels the timeline of *Flight from Reason*.

Made in the USA
San Bernardino, CA
15 September 2016